# Walking the War Zones of Pakistan

*One Woman's Journey into the Shadow of the Taliban*

*To Ken & Sandy*
*Ruth Anne Kocour*
*3/29/12*

# Walking the War Zones of Pakistan

*One Woman's Journey into the Shadow of the Taliban*

## Ruth Anne Kocour

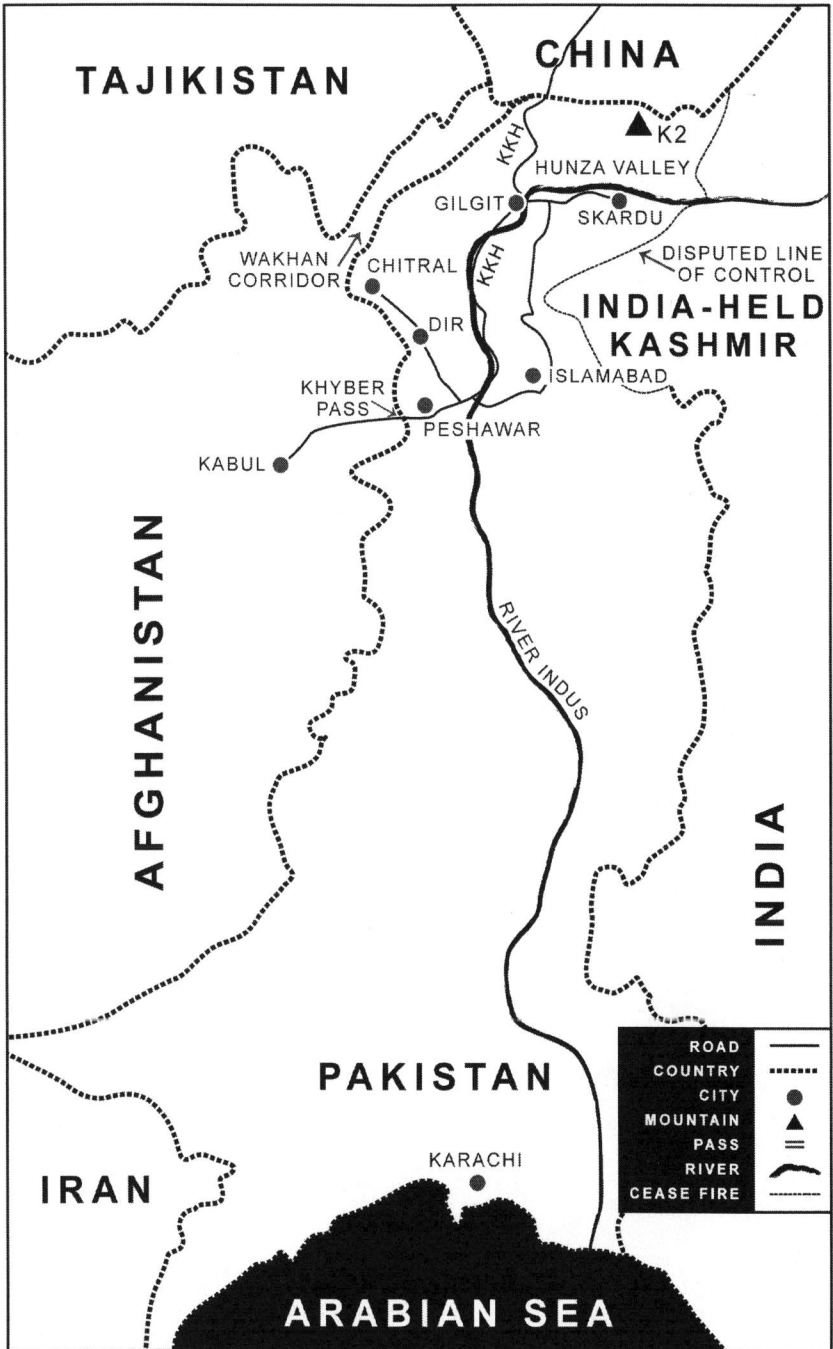

*MAPS ARE APPROXIMATE

*SOME OF THE BORDERS SHOWN ON THIS MAP ARE DISPUTED.

*Overview of Pakistan*

# Contents

# AUTHOR'S NOTE AND ACKNOWLEDGMENTS

This chronicle was taken from my own voice recordings, personal journals, and notes made during my treks in northern Pakistan and areas surrounding K2. Some individuals' names have been changed. All photos, including those on the cover, were taken by me and are my property. Stacey Foltz rendered the maps.

A special thank you to the following people for their insights and suggestions: Mary and Nazir Ansari, Julie Conover, Tony DeRonnebeck, Bob Dowling, Donna Ducharme, Debbie Martin, Chris Price, Ron Randolf-Wall, Dr. Beverly Whipple, Allegra Atkinson Willison, and my patient and supportive husband, Bob.

## OTHER BOOKS BY RUTH ANNE KOCOUR

*Facing the Extreme*

*"To go to Pakistan, you need patience."*
                                    *—A Pakistani friend*

*"To go to Pakistan, you need anesthetizing."*
                                    *—An American friend*

# I.

# BE SMART, BE BRAVE, BE AFRAID

*I felt singled out, an object of curiosity and contempt. Instinctively my hand reached for the veil I wore out of respect, never expecting to cling to it for security. Pulling it higher around my face, I felt the full impact of being six feet tall, blonde, blue-eyed, and American.*

## Islamabad, Pakistan

### September 1998

The United States had just evacuated its diplomatic corps from Islamabad. Islamic terrorists had bombed U.S. embassies in Kenya and Tanzania. The United States had retaliated, firing upon the Afghanistan stronghold of Osama bin Laden. Pakistan had detonated its first nuclear test explosion, sending diplomatic shockwaves across India to the West. Sadly, personal friend and writer/adventurer Ned Gillette had just been gunned down in the very region of northern Pakistan where I was now headed.

So why was I in Pakistan?

To see K2, the second highest mountain on earth. Not to climb it; I'd already climbed enough mountains. By all accounts, this would be a long and difficult trek, up the Baltoro Glacier to a place called Concordia, where two of the world's largest glaciers converge at the base of K2 in Pakistan-held Kashmir. In talking with other mountaineers, one issue always came up: porters in Pakistan were volatile and unreliable—climbers told of being robbed and left to die. But I had been in communication with my guide in Pakistan for several years and remained convinced he could run such an expedition.

While political tensions within Pakistan escalated over religious allegiance and war with India, my desire to go there remained firm. Out on a glacier in a remote corner of Pakistan, I'd be far from strife and unrest, I told myself. With the situation in Pakistan deteriorating, if I were ever to see K2, it had to be now or never.

*Never* would have been the choice of family and friends. People were worried sick that I might really do this. In a last-ditch effort to dissuade me, my husband came up with headlines like these: PAKISTAN'S RADICAL GROUPS VOW TO KIDNAP AMERICANS IF CLINTON DOES NOT APOLOGIZE FOR MISSILE ATTACKS ON AFGHANISTAN; AMERICANS WARNED TO LEAVE PAKISTAN; TERRORIST STRIKE IN PAKISTAN IMMINENT. One friend even printed a page from the Taliban Web site—it promoted throwing acid in the faces of unveiled women.

"Be smart, be brave, be afraid," another friend simply advised.

As my travel plans took shape, everyone realized I couldn't be talked out of this. "Ruth Anne, if you must go to Pakistan, blend!" a fashion-conscious friend insisted. Taking my cue from her words, my first stop in London, during my layover between flights to Islamabad, was the Pakistani district. I needed the traditional garb worn by women in Pakistan, called a *salwar kameez,* a three-piece affair consisting of a long veil and tent-like dress with baggy pants worn underneath, all intended to conceal the contours of a woman's body. These ensembles came in one size: one-size-fits-all. One-size-fits-all is fine, unless you're six feet tall in a culture that isn't. I tried on a set, just to be safe, and checked out my new look in the shop's mirror. Between my height and my blond hair, I looked like a walking lighthouse, even in a veil. Having no other options, I bought the somewhat short salwar kameez anyway.

Feeling ridiculous in my billowing Pakistani pants and dress, which could have doubled as a parachute, and already annoyed by my veil, I arrived at London's Gatwick Airport for my continuing flight to Islamabad. At the check-in counter, I inquired about conditions in Pakistan. The British gentleman manning the desk grew red as he answered: "Things are horrendous there, just horrendous! Terrorists are targeting English and American people. It's very, very dangerous!"

Undeterred, I proceeded out the concourse. I was on my way to K2, and I wasn't turning back. When I reached my gate, I felt more at ease. The few other women there (Pakistani) wore garb much like mine, and the men had on the male version of a salwar kameez, which looks like pajamas with a knee-length shirt.

Once onboard, I didn't remove my veil. It was do-as-they-do: the Muslim women kept their veils on; I did, too. But throughout the flight, mine kept slipping off, and the closer we came to our destination, the more naked I felt every time it did. By the time we landed, I'd developed a sixth sense, *veil awareness*, and automatically grabbed my veil every time it crept back on my head.

The airport in Islamabad with its throng of bearded males, all dressed traditionally and all conspicuously leery of me, was the most foreign and unsettling place I'd ever been. Then, I noticed a clean-shaven man wearing new blue jeans and an ice-blue Polo shirt, the same color as his eyes. When we spotted one another, we both laughed, realizing we'd dressed for each other's culture. This was Ziad, the guide who would lead me up the Baltoro Glacier to K2. Until now, I'd only communicated with him by mail.

Ziad limped and walked with a cane, not exactly what I expected of the man who'd accompany me to the second-highest mountain on earth. Yet, Ziad had just returned from K2 base camp. While he was climbing a pass adjacent to K2, an ice wall had collapsed directly in front of him. The avalanche swept him over two hundred yards down a gully, knocking him unconscious. When he came to, he saw a porter near him, dead and in pieces. It took Ziad fourteen hours to crawl down the mountainside and out onto the Baltoro Glacier. Not until five days later did a military helicopter spot and rescue him. Ziad swore he would never return to K2. But not to worry; his brother Majid would guide me to the base of K2 in his place.

Everyone in Pakistan has a *brother*, I would soon learn. There, brother means of the same family, the same tribe. But for the moment, I took the term literally.

At my hotel, Ziad attended to check-in while I waited in a reception area. On the coffee table, a local newspaper featured a lead story about a Pakistani woman who'd worked for an American company in Islamabad. She'd been found dead—beheaded—and officials were still searching for her head.

Welcome tea was served.

From our hotel, we drove to a government complex to meet the Minister of Expeditions, who "carried a warm spot in his heart for Americans, having been educated as a boy at a private school run by an American couple." After dispensing with niceties, he began a long tutorial he seemed eager to deliver. "The area around K2 is restricted, a strategically sensitive military zone near the disputed Line of Control, where the war over Kashmir is being fought with India. You must adhere to a mandatory itinerary, camp only at designated campsites, and you will be required to clear military check stations along the way." Pulling one document from his thick stack of forms, he held it up. "This authorization is for a helicopter. In case of emergency, it will come for you quickly." More accurately, I would be *eligible* for helicopter evacuation, at a price—four thousand dollars, U.S.—and weather permitting. But based on Ziad's rescue, I knew not to count on fast evacuation, in any event.

Assuming an air of importance, the minister signed each and every paper. "If there is anything I am an expert in, it is writing my own name." Laughing at his own joke, he wished me good-bye and good luck. Turning somber, he added, "Tell no one you are American."

The next morning, I met my new guide, Ziad's blood brother, Majid. He bowed stiffly and remained silent. Majid's fair skin, sandy-brown hair, and green eyes looked more Western than Pakistani, and his gaunt, pale frame looked anything but guide-like. Majid remained so uncomfortably silent, I wondered about spending the upcoming month with him. But when we arrived at the domestic airport, he began to open up.

As we walked across the tarmac to a circa World War II plane, Majid quietly joked, "We locals say PIA (Pakistan International Airlines) stands for *Prayers in the Air.* Some say it means, *Please Inform Allah.*" We would fly north to Skardu, the capital of Baltistan and a Shiite region in northern Pakistan. There, we would pick up ground transportation to take us to the starting point of our trek.

It was a full flight—all locals, all male. The engines rumbled to a start; we bumped down the runway, waiting for liftoff. Airborne, we climbed northward over tiers of ever-higher peaks. Even at cruising altitude, the mountaintops were at eye level. Once aloft, the captain invited me into the cockpit to photograph Nanga Parbat, the ninth-highest mountain in the world. "In Pakistan, clouds are made of rock," the pilot said, laughing. But it was no joke—we were clearly navigating around, not over, mountain peaks.

Soon, through a corridor of red-and-purple mountains, a sand-dune–covered valley came into sight. When our plane banked to the left, I could look directly down onto the Indus River snaking between sandbars and ledges of gravel. Our final approach required a tight, spiral descent to avoid hitting rock walls twenty thousand feet high. The aircraft leveled out only long enough to touch down.

After clearing airport security, Majid and I piled into a hired jeep and rattled down a poplar-lined dirt road while our driver swerved to avoid animals, schoolchildren, and donkey carts. Judging by the locals' quick reactions, the right-of-way went to the largest vehicle, driven the fastest. We arrived at our hotel, which was perched on a cliff overlooking the Indus River.

Majid saw to my check in and cautioned, "Please, you are not to leave the hotel without me. Also, I must insist. From now on, you cannot say you are American, and do not speak with an American accent. I must go now to finalize arrangements for tomorrow. You are quite safe here."

At midnight, a loud clatter shook me awake—an earthquake, I thought. Leaping from bed, I groped for the light switch. But when I flicked it on, nothing happened. The rattling and banging ended, but not the power outage. Again, I told myself: *once we're out on the glacier, everything will be fine.*

At breakfast, the hotel manager confirmed my suspicion: indeed, it had been an earthquake. But he expressed no more concern than had it been an afternoon rain shower. "This is quite common here, madam. We are used to it." *I guess I'll have to get used to it too,* I thought. Now, sipping tea and gazing across the Indus to the mountains beyond, I was glad I'd come this far. I really was going to K2.

"Our driver and jeep have come for us," Majid said, popping into the dining room. "Please, we must go now." I followed Majid outside, adjusting my veil for the long ride to the starting point of our trek. Majid gestured toward the jeep's backseat, where curtains completely covered the windows, preventing sight of any passenger, namely me. "Ruth, you will sit there, please." Meanwhile, Majid and our driver climbed into the front. As the jeep jerked forward, Majid turned to me and said, "And now we begin our interesting and exciting drive."

*MAPS ARE APPROXIMATE

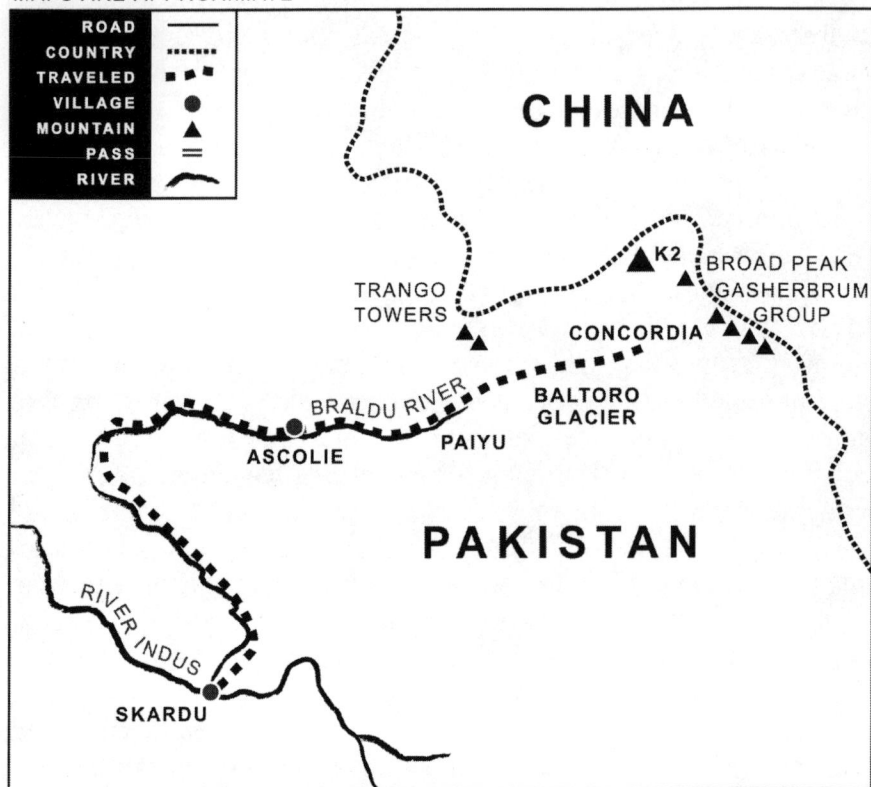

*Route traveled to Concordia and K2 from Skardu in Pakistan*

Passing through outlying villages, other motorized vehicles became increasingly infrequent, rendering us all the more conspicuous, particularly with Majid's Otis Redding tape blasting on the jeep's tape deck. Skillfully, our driver navigated a jeep trail alongside the Indus River, where an opening had been blasted through the canyon wall to make way for the scant road. We skirted pot holes large enough to swallow an entire car and places where the river had undercut the bank beneath the road, causing it to break off in chunks. Curtains blocked my view, but I didn't need to see out the windows to know what was happening. Every time we skirted a dangerous place, Majid leaned hard, in the opposite direction, sometimes onto our driver. Judging by his body language, we must have been passing sheer drop-offs the entire way. We didn't slow down.

For the better part of the day, we followed the Indus River upstream toward its tributary, the Braldu River. Originating in the glaciers of northern Pakistan, the Indus drains an area the size of Texas and flows southeast into India, its namesake. As early as 3000 BC, the Indus cradled civilizations, as migratory people brought new cultures, thought, languages, and religions to regions along its course.

*Inshallah* (God willing) has to be the most frequently used word in Urdu, Pakistan's national language. The worse the road, the more our driver muttered *Inshallah*. My neck ached from the sudden downs and ups, jerking side to side, and from having the luggage fly forward, hitting me in the back of my head. After six bone-jarring hours, we climbed one last pass, coincidently named Inshallah Pass. From there, we made our final descent to the village of Ascolie, located on an alluvial fan adjacent to the Braldu River, at an elevation of ten thousand feet. From Ascolie, we would walk seventy miles to the Baltoro Glacier and then traverse thirty-nine miles of ice to reach Concordia, at the base of K2. After years of planning and a week of travelling to reach this point, our foot journey would begin here, on the outskirts of a remote village, where the road abruptly ended.

*The village of Ascolie*

I hopped from the jeep, happy to stand on firm ground. In the evening light, I studied the small, sparsely wooded glen, which would be our first government-designated campsite. Two vehicles had preceded us: one carried supplies, the other our Balti porters—Shiite Muslims, descended from Tibetans, who long ago made their way westward across the Himalaya. I counted seventeen men in total.

"This seems like a lot of porters," I said to Majid.

"We cannot use animals to carry supplies where we are going. So this number of men is needed for the trek up the glacier, Ruth. These are all my brothers—we are from the same family. You will be safe with them."

When Majid announced our arrival, our entire crew stopped what they were doing and stood at attention. Older men and teen-aged boys fell into line. For the first time since entering this country, I stood face-to-face with a group of men who looked me in the eye and grinned. As Majid made introductions, each man jumped forward, took my hand in both of his, and bowed. Some were shy, though pleased to have their turn, with broad smiles showing from behind thick black mustaches and beards. Their foreign names ran together in a slur of Urdu until I had met each man.

"These porters are happy to be here. With so many cancellations by expeditions, they are grateful for any opportunity to work," Majid explained.

The porters scattered and resumed their tasks, which, judging by the results, had occupied them for hours. A waft of curry hung in the air—they'd already erected a cook tent, with dinner on the stove. Spotting the massive pile of storage barrels and wooden boxes our porters would have to carry, I voiced my concern. "Majid, how can these men possibly haul all this gear?"

"Ruth, the law protects porters. They cannot carry over twenty-five kilos (fifty-five pounds) and must not be forced to walk more than the legally regulated schedule each day," Majid answered.

Still, the men seemed ill-equipped. Most wore tattered low-cut gym shoes, laced with bits of twine, and I would soon learn they didn't have tents. Instead, they would spend their nights—even on the glacier—crammed together under plastic tarps to stay warm and relatively dry. "Porters do not own tents," Majid explained. "Trekking and climbing parties are required by law to provide tarps, because these porters cannot afford to buy them."

"We have put your things here, among these Junipers," Majid said, leading me into a nearby grove of trees. For us, these trees are holy. We burn their branches as a blessing because we believe the smoke carries the voice of God. Now please, join me for tea."

Following Majid's example, I removed my boots before entering the cook tent. As soon as our cook, Ismail, arrived with teapot and cups, Majid pulled out a battery of medications. "Yes, I am fighting typhoid. I picked it up a month ago, when I ate an apple in the bazaar. The next day my body felt like a dead rock. My parents were so worried—they sacrificed a buffalo, sheep, and chickens. I am supposed to be home, in bed. But with Ziad injured, this is quite impossible. I will have to take it easy on the trek."

*All the better ... I didn't come here to run to K2,* I thought.

The next day was perfect—calm and sunny—with lots of activity in camp as our porters prepared to trek. I dressed in hiking clothes—a long-sleeve shirt and slacks. Even here, where junipers outnumbered people, there was no place in this cover-up culture for shorts or tee shirts. Majid came to breakfast wearing a turban, but he had abandoned his salwar kameez for Western trekking clothes. Eating quickly, he excused himself to help our porters get ready to leave.

Outside, two porters shouldered either end of a pine sapling while Majid hung a metal scale from the center point. Each man lined up to witness the weighing of his own load to make sure it fell within the legally mandated limit. The porters secured loads to their backs, using frayed hemp rope and crude wooden frames padded with burlap. Balancing a fifty-pound storage barrel on one's back didn't look easy. I'd be carrying my own pack but not nearly the weight these men would carry. While Ismail and his helper broke down the kitchen, Majid spurred our porters into action.

In the clear morning light, we began moving up the Braldu River basin that ultimately would become glacier. I settled into a relaxed gait, relieved to finally be trekking. Slowly and steadily, we worked our way along an expansive swath of pebbles, deposited by the Braldu River. As we gained elevation, the flood plain narrowed to a steep gorge, intensifying the reverberation of rushing water. With spring runoff behind us, the water level had dropped, exposing rock caverns carved by the same forces that had scoured the terrain of vegetation. River rock, propelled from upstream, littered the route, an indication that during periods of high water, this entire basin turned into a swollen torrent.

Midway through the day, we came to a wobbly structure dangling high above the river. "This bridge is a recent advancement," Majid said. "People used to cross here in boats made from animal skins. It is a good bridge—some bridges go unrepaired until they break."

The good bridge consisted of crude wooden planks, positioned loosely across two rusted cables, anchored by boulders on either side of the gorge. An old man stood guard to keep people from stealing parts. He maintained the bridge by swapping out old planks with new boards he had hewn. It turned out to be a toll bridge; to cross, we had to pay a few rupees to cover his salary and expenses.

*Bridge keeper*

With every step the planks shifted, while the bridge sank and rebounded trampoline-like. Focusing on the frothy water below, I loosened my pack to jettison it, if necessary. Once we had all crossed, Majid told how a porter had once tumbled off this same bridge and drowned before anyone could save him.

Slogging up a seemingly endless slope of loose gravel, we came to a terrace of cultivated fields surrounded by rock walls. Here, we encountered our first military checkpoint, set within a tiny enclave where chickens and goats foraged freely in, on, and around flat-roofed huts. I sat in a little barnyard, watching a soldier complete his flurry of rubber stamping and paperwork. Meanwhile, Majid bought a few last-minute provisions, a flapping rooster and a goat on a rope, looking straight up … at me. I couldn't return the gaze: *dead goat walking,* I thought.

"I have paid too much for the goat, but only because this will be our last chance to buy," Majid groused.

For several days, we made our way through the Braldu River gorge, the only passageway to the Baltoro Glacier. The ground was so unstable in some places that we had to spread out to keep the loose slope from giving way under our weight. Above us, conglomerated rock, mortared together by mud, broke loose with regularity, sending boulders plummeting down onto the route. With good reason, locals had named this the Bombing Range. We hustled past a spot where three porters had died the year before when a rainstorm had set off a rockslide. "They were told not to camp close to the wall, but they did it anyway," Majid mused.

By mid-afternoon, we'd arrived to a sand embankment above the river, a violent and noisy place, where canyon winds roared over the sound of rapids. At times, I could even hear the clunking of boulders bouncing along underwater. The surrounding mountains looked like cathedral spires, sharp and jagged. We would spend the night here.

*Karakoram skyline*

During dinner, Majid spoke of family values in his culture: "When parents retire from their family obligations, the oldest brother takes over the financial and educational needs of younger members, especially sisters. Depending on how well he can provide, this can extend as far as cousins. Even if his sisters marry, the oldest brother will provide for them. During moments of happiness and sorrow, we all stand by each other. We are what we call a hand-to-hand culture."

The following morning, we awoke to pounding rain. *The only thing worse than trekking all the way to Concordia in bad weather would be to arrive there, and not see K2,* I thought. But by the time we started out, the rain had turned to light drizzle. *Now if winter will only hold off ...*

Majid, feeling weak, needed to go slowly. As we moved along, our porters sang broken-heart songs, "part of our tradition," according to Majid. Within a few hours, we came up against a near-vertical wall, two thousand feet high, known as the Cliff. At the base stood a small tent with a pick leaning against it where a villager stayed in order to repair the trail. Where a pick couldn't do the job, dried junipers had been jammed into cracks in the wall and covered with rock and mud to serve as improvised walkways. "One time, this German guy turned to jelly and fell off," Majid recalled of these high ramps. "When we managed to get him back up, he blacked out from fear." I couldn't imagine dragging a limp body across those spindly structures.

I watched anxiously as our porters started out across the path of wet, slippery rocks, their loads bumping and snagging on rock overhangs, throwing them off balance. When it was my turn, I tried to avoid looking straight down at the river through gaps in the ramps. Instead, I paid close attention to every step in front of me. Any momentary loss of concentration—or simply a foot placed carelessly—could be my last step. The route descended in a slippery mud-and-boulder pitch, ending in the river itself. We had to wade through thigh-deep water until we found a level place to climb out.

After days of hiking, climbing, slipping, and sliding, we had made it as far as Paiyu, elevation 11,220 feet, our last campsite before moving onto the Baltoro Glacier. From Paiyu, we had a panoramic view looking upstream. Between immense lateral moraines of gravel lay a floodplain, where the river meandered through exposed sandbars in slow-moving braids. Just beyond, the Baltoro Glacier ended in an ugly gray pile of ice and rock, which had taken centuries to reach this place. Above the glacier towered the saw-tooth Karakoram mountain range, with eight peaks over twenty-five thousand feet.

*Karakoram peaks and the Baltoro Glacier viewed from Paiyu*

Our first afternoon at Paiyu, I noticed a fresh pelt drying on a boulder. It looked disturbingly like the goat Majid had bought in Ascolie. When I inquired, Majid quickly explained that this blood sacrifice was customary before tackling the glacier—the porters required it to ensure their safety. "Here we give thanks to Allah before we slaughter any animal. This is done often in our culture. When a family reaches twelve males, we also sacrifice a goat to share with the poor."

Our porters spent the afternoon preparing for their goat festival, to be held later in the evening. One man was tuning his flute while others butchered different portions of goat. I found it only minimally consoling that every part would be put to good use.

"May I *attention* you!" Majid summoned me to the cook tent where Ismail presented the feast he had created for this special occasion: leg of goat, vegetables in pastry, lentils, and *chapatti* (traditional flatbread). He had even gathered a bouquet of wildflowers as a centerpiece. To add to the festivities, Majid broke out his portable tape player and a selection of his favorite Pakistani tunes. New batteries would have improved the sound—the music droned on in what sounded like a slow rendition of "Itsy-Bitsy Spider."

After a while, Majid, in a cheerful mood, gave the tape player a rest and broke into lively conversation. "When I was young, I considered becoming a Fundamentalist. Because I was strong, I was invited to Afghanistan to fight with the Mujahidin. But my father would not let me do it. He said I had to stay at home with the family. Some of my friends who did go now have senior positions within the Taliban."

Majid entertained me with more tunes while I sipped tea and waited for the festival to begin. Nothing happened. Having never attended a goat festival, I wondered if simply eating goat constituted the event, in which case I'd already had my festival. Or maybe this would be a late night festival? Between inhaling smoke from the oil lamp and straining to follow the foreign melodies, I'd had enough. A little festival goes a long way—I excused myself, knowing all ordinary dinner parties would be downhill from here.

My festival never happened. The men had been waiting for me, the woman, to go to bed. Then, the action kicked into full swing with singing, dancing, storytelling, and flute playing ... all night long.

The beat picked up—I was trying to develop an ear for their music, without success. I wondered if this was one long song, or a series of mini-songs. With sleep out of the question, I listened, and reviewed the trip so far: The guide I originally hired nearly died on this glacier and refused to ever return. Instead, he sent his typhoid-infected brother, who should be home in bed, and has high-ranking friends in the Taliban. Now, our porters have sacrificed a goat to keep them safe on the glacier. What's to worry about?

In the morning, the usual wake-up sounds—coughing, chopping, and clattering—began later than usual. Breakfast consisted of goat leftovers seasoned with dried mulberries. Majid showed up in a terrible mood. "The political situation and global propaganda has hurt our tourist industry so much, the clients we worked years to develop are disappearing. So far this year, twenty mountaineering expeditions have cancelled trips to K2 due to unrest and negative publicity. These days, I even have to worry about my own white skin because people here think I am not Pakistani. If things get any worse, we will have to find jobs outside of guiding—maybe sell bottled water or go into mining," he growled.

We ate quickly to get a jump on the day. Outside, I scanned the horizon for any sign of unsettled weather but saw only a few ravens riding wind drafts above. We moved out and headed toward the Baltoro Glacier, which took on new dimensions as we neared. The glacier appeared to be four stories tall and a mile wide. We crossed floodplain and scrambled up a wall of ice and rock. Once on top, the glacier fanned out in beautiful monotony, like a sea of immense waves, frozen mid-storm. Eons ago, a sea did cover this entire area, the Mesozoic Tethys Sea. When the Asian and Indian subcontinents collided, the resulting near-vertical thrust of tectonic plates produced the Karakoram mountain range, which today is rising faster than erosion can wear it down.

*Surface of the Baltoro Glacier*

Think of glaciers as frozen rivers. Propelled by gravity and sheer weight, glaciers flow downward, ramming bedrock and cutting ravines as they pass. When glaciers collide with immovable obstacles, they bend and strain, forcing cracks, called crevasses, to open on their surfaces. Where glaciers have to squeeze through narrow passages, unstable compression ridges of ice slabs stack up like dominoes, poised to collapse without warning. Under the ice, rivers resulting from pressure and friction erode tunnels and force their way through.

The glacier seemed alive; it was quiet in the morning but noisy after the sun had warmed things up. At night, with my head resting against the glacier, I could hear tumbling water, and the banging and scraping of boulders and ice chunks being swept through passageways below. For two weeks, we would walk on ice, sleep on ice, and drink water melted from ice.

The glacier moved constantly, causing the route to shift or disappear from one day to another. There was always a sense of groundlessness—nothing safe to hang onto. Solid-looking footholds collapsed beneath our feet, forcing frequent detours. Zigzagging to find secure routes, we had to jump over crevasses we couldn't avoid—in some places others blocked our way altogether. There were squeezers: cracks that narrow as they descend, wedging victims so tightly that their own body heat causes them to inch down further and further until finally a last breath is impossible. Even more insidious were little chinks or slits in the glacier's surface. These could break open, exposing dome-shaped caverns with walls impossible to scale.

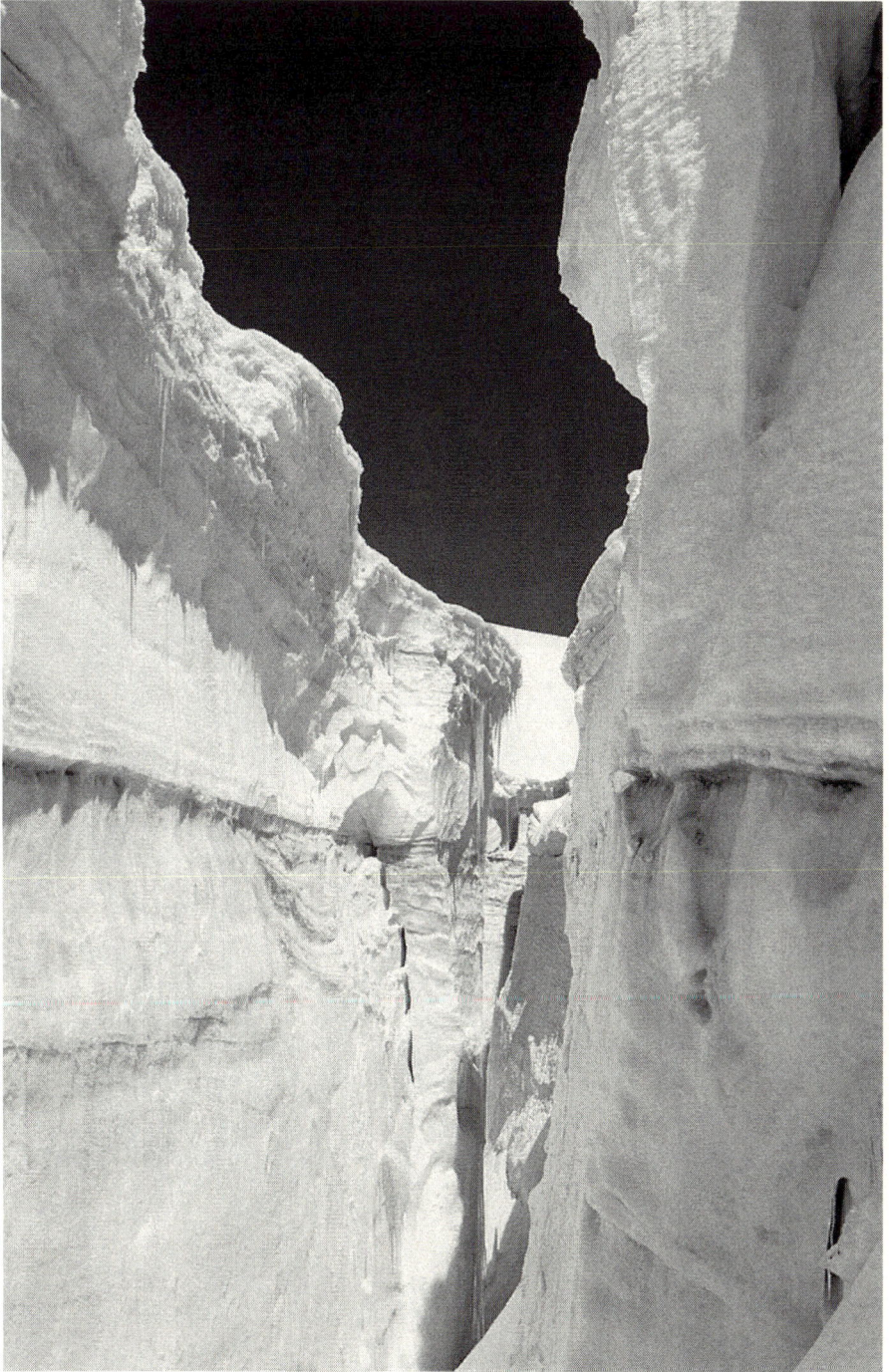

*View from inside a squeezer crevasse*

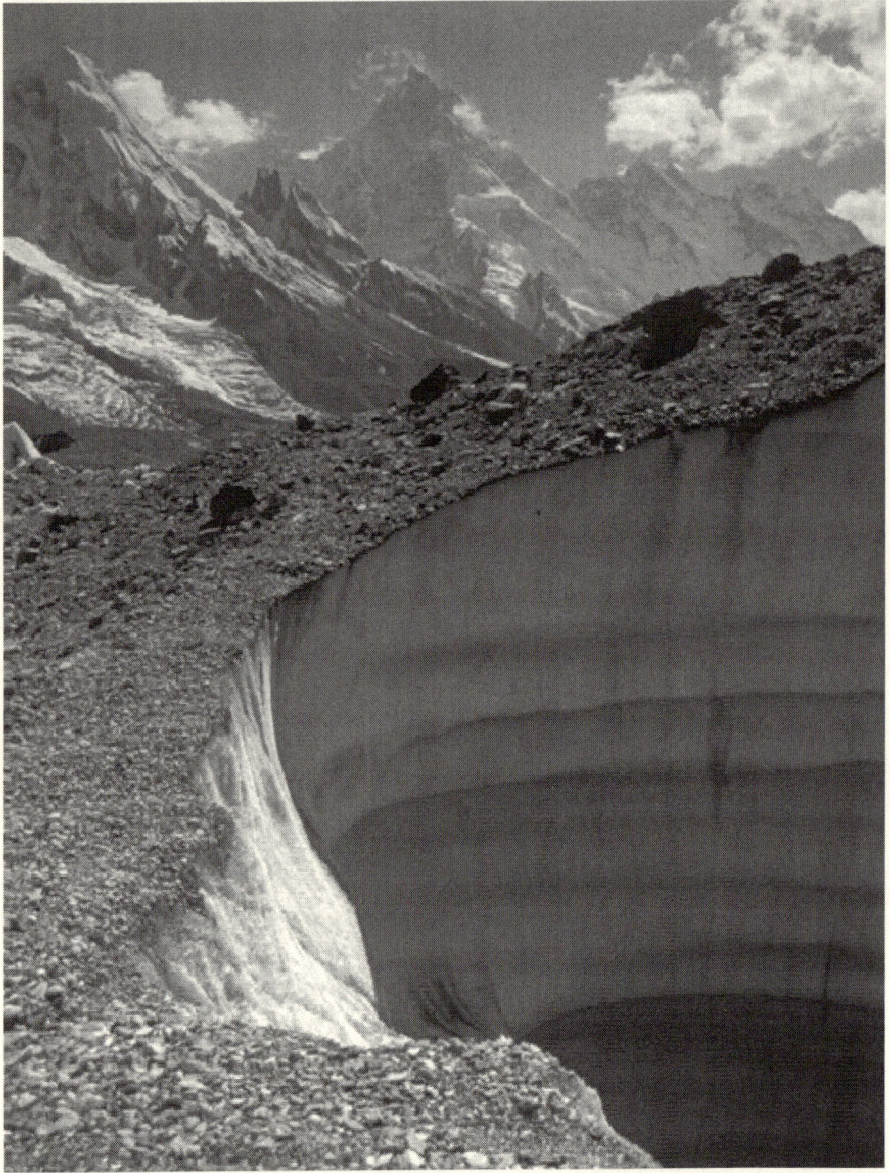

*A dome-shaped crevasse has broken open, exposing striations of rock deposited on the glacier's surface during previous seasons.*

The entire place felt like a chapter from Genesis. A thin layer of black-and-gray dirt gave the glacier's surface a lurid, subterranean appearance, as though here, the earth had been eviscerated. Gigantic boulders balanced precariously on free-standing pedestals of ice, like huge mushroom caps. Moat-like troughs of melt water encircled other rocks, some expanding to murky sinkholes, the size of small lakes. Even the mountains looked as though they'd just risen from deep within the earth, especially the Great Trango Tower, a monolith of granite 20,608 feet high.

*A boulder has shielded the ice from the sun's rays, leaving it perched on a free-standing stalk of ice.*

*The Great Trango Tower (20,608')*

We retreated further into the ice age. Centuries-old ice overhung ridges, threatening to fall, while cataclysmic avalanches thundered down without warning, scouring mountainsides and leaving rock exposed. One slide had swept across the glacier and ended up piled against the opposite mountainside. I'd stood above avalanches on mountains in the Himalaya and Alaska, and felt the pull of suction as snow slabs broke away. I'd felt the ground shake on impact and seen tents blown to shreds by resulting wind blasts. I had a healthy respect for these forces.

Once we were safely out on the glacier, Majid seemed to loosen up. "I am glad America bombed the stronghold of Osama bin Laden. That guy needed a dose! Those extremist guys use Islam to hide behind and give all Muslims a bad name. Many Muslims are upset about these radical guys and their effect on our world image. Those guys call us *brothers*—I do not need this type of brother!"

Majid continued, his mood darkening and verging on despair: "I have seen all the preparation for the New Millennium on the Internet. The world is marching forward into a new century while Pakistan is going backward—we are being left behind, in dust. Our government does nothing for us—it has no money," he said.

"What do people of Pakistan most want?" I asked.

"A job!" he replied.

*A job—a chance to participate in today's world. To have a job is to have freedom, purpose. Without jobs, people fall victim to crime, terrorism, slavery, and drug dealers.*

What did Majid most want? I asked.

"To go to Las Vegas! I have seen the video," he said, perking up.

For dinner, Ismail served goat meatballs on spaghetti. While we ate, Majid digressed about politics, and his government's recent detonation of nuclear devices. "Our people were not aware of any nuclear testing until thirty-six hours before the tests took place. There were three above-ground blasts and three underground, in the mountains south of Islamabad. But I do not understand why we get all this bad publicity. Your country has the violent culture! You have drive-by shootings! You have drugs and teen pregnancies! I have seen this on televisions in hotel lobbies."

He paused, deep in thought. "But all Muslim countries are in trouble, which makes me wonder if the problem lies with us, not with the rest of the world. Muslim countries have an assembly, where they come together to discuss issues and vote. But they have no control over terrorists—in this, they are powerless."

To my surprise, Majid then brought up the Ned Gillette murder. When I told him I had known Ned, this unexpected blow horrified him. "No, Ruth! Is this really true?"

"Yes, Majid, do you know any details?" I asked.

"No, but one of our porters is from the village where the murder took place. I will go speak with him now," he said, shaking his head and rushing from the cook tent. I felt bad this news had hit him so hard.

The porter seemed terrified and refused to talk, Majid later told me. I didn't press the subject.

Once back outside, the proportion of our surroundings again hit me. Such appalling perpendicularity—in all directions, mountains virtually filled the sky. Sunbeams streamed between ragged peaks, and massive ice blocks leaned on each other like drunken sailors, their dark shadows swallowing up our camp. Our tents, tiny in this setting, reminded me of sailboats, cast about between ghostly, titanic icebergs. What physical and psychological isolation early explorers must have endured!

I crawled into the false security of my tent's frail structure. As soon as I'd settled in, the ground shook, and I heard a roar from some not-too-distant place. I tried to gauge from the combined sound of mass, power, and velocity whether we were in the immediate path of a landslide. A full five minutes later, the last boulders bounced to a stop.

Early the next morning, another loud noise roused me, this time the rumbling and *phwap, phwap, phwap* of a helicopter. When the aircraft roared overhead, I saw the words PAKISTAN ARMY painted on its side. This Russian-made helicopter hauled supplies to army posts on the frontier, according to Majid. "Here, we are very close to China, India, and Afghanistan. In fact, half of K2 lies in China and the other half in Pakistan. Only a short distance from here, the war over Kashmir is being fought with India. The Line of Control is just down this glacier." How ironic that an area once proposed for an international peace park now served as the highest battlefield on earth. But there's more to this conflict: within these glaciers lies Pakistan's wealth, control over the watershed of the Indus River. The helicopter dwindled to a speck, vanishing into the labyrinth of mountains and ice.

We were not alone, even on the ice. One afternoon, while picking our way along the glacier's edge, we came around a mountain spur and heard a voice shout out something in Urdu. Seconds later, I saw a camouflage screen draped over the entrance to a cave only thirty feet away. Through the screen, I could make out a soldier crouched behind a machine gun, aimed directly at us. Majid yelled back—the soldier emerged, machine gun still pointed our way. After Majid presented permits, the conversation became somewhat more relaxed. Soon, we were on our way again.

*No more surprises*, I thought, focusing my eyes ahead.

Not long after, I spotted more motion on the ice as two soldiers came barreling down on us, dressed totally in white. Everything from their hats, goggles, backpacks, and fatigues—even their boots were white. They looked like space warriors. Each soldier carried three white rifles, two slung over the shoulders and another worn cross-chest. Again, Majid presented papers. As luck would have it, one of these soldiers had assisted in Ziad's rescue from the glacier. When they learned Majid was Ziad's brother, they embraced him like family.

Saying good-bye, we marched forward, taking a serpentine path between crevasses and icefalls. As the sun heated the glacier's surface, making it slick in some places and mushy in others, our progress slowed. Only the occasional crash of a distant avalanche punctuated the sound of our boots scraping across or breaking through ice. Meanwhile, I kept scanning the glacier for activity. Sure enough, two figures came into view, tiny in the far distance. They looked almost insect-like as they navigated around hazards invisible to us—at times, disappearing altogether between undulations in the ice.

When the two specters reached us—men, not insects—they stopped to talk. They were civilians, a guide and his client. Majid knew the guide. His client, an Iranian living in California, told us he planned to cross over the Khyber Pass into Afghanistan after leaving the Baltoro Glacier. I asked how he intended to pull it off. "I'm carrying U.S., Iranian, and Afghan passports," he replied. "I look the part and speak the language fluently. Since I worked as a photojournalist in Afghanistan during the war, I have friends there who will hide me. I should be OK, provided the authorities don't catch me."

*And I thought I was on an adventure ...*

That night, Majid showed up for dinner with a solemn expression on his face. After a long pause, he began. "I have spoken more with our porter about the murder of your friend. He is too afraid to say much, but this is what he told me. Your friend camped in a place where he was warned not to go, a restricted tribal area, where foreigners must have special permission and a local guide. Two villagers tried to tell your friend he had to leave—one even offered to guide him. Your friend refused; an argument broke out. Later in the night, those same men returned and fired a shotgun at the tent where your friend was sleeping. Our government demanded an inquiry, but the local magistrate was so terrified of an international incident, he refused to do it. The villagers thought the U.S. would bomb them, just like it bombed the stronghold of Osama bin Laden. So Islamabad sent high-level officials to find the murderers. It took two weeks before the criminals were arrested and taken to Islamabad. I am quite sure they have been hanged by now."

I thanked Majid and stepped outside, just as an unearthly band of light swept across the glacier, giving the mountains a surreal appearance. The farther up the glacier I looked, the more the peaks obliterated the horizon—many topped out at two miles above the glacier. For me, geology had once involved imagination—here, it exceeded imagination.

The next morning, Majid swapped his turban for a brimmed hat, fashioned like a cowboy hat, and pulled out his favorite Willie Nelson tape. I wondered how "On the Road Again" would sound on his tape player with its low batteries. Headset and hat in place, he took the lead, while our team strung out behind. I dubbed him the Karakoram Cowboy.

The day dragged on. To pass time, Majid reviewed the previous climbing season: "Last year many climbers died in the Karakoram. First, two Koreans and a French couple vanished on Broad Peak. Then, a team of twenty-one Japanese hired six hundred porters to carry everything from telecommunication equipment to luxuries from the homeland into Gasherbrum base camp. Seven climbers made it to the top—four disappeared and were never found. On K2, six Japanese summited and returned safely to base camp. After a celebration dinner, they went to sleep. And while they enjoyed the sweet dreams of success, an earthquake set off an avalanche, crushing them. Their porters gave them a mountaineer's burial, dropping the dead into a crevasse. Thirty minutes later a helicopter came for the bodies. The porters tried to recover their buried clients, but could not. The crevasse was too deep."

*What's the point if you don't come back alive? Too often rescues turn into body recoveries. How easy to wander off out here and never be seen again.*

"Majid, have you ever been on this glacier during an earthquake?" I asked.

"Yes, twice. It sounds like bombs going off under the ice."

*Bombs ... under the ice.* At that very moment, an ice wall, roughly thirty feet high, collapsed onto the path we'd just crossed. The impact sounded like a bomb. No one uttered a word.

Late in the day, we came upon a rock hut set in the middle of the glacier. It was a tiny one-room military outpost, manned by a handful of Pakistani soldiers. As soon as we arrived, Majid disappeared inside the hut, leaving our porters to unload. He emerged after staying so long; I asked if there was a problem. "Oh no, I know these guys. We were just sitting around the table *gospering* (gossiping). We will camp here tonight. Tomorrow will be an easy day."

It was thirty-two degrees inside my tent when I awoke the next morning—fairly warm, considering we were above fifteen thousand feet. This also happened to be the day my Hostess Cupcakes expired.

No kidding. Before I left home, a friend had slipped them into my duffle, knowing how surprised I'd be when I discovered them. "Enjoy by September 13, 1998," the package read. Despite being flattened to the thickness of pancakes, they still tasted fantastic.

Majid showed up for breakfast wearing his Karakoram cowboy hat, wraparound shades, and a hot-pink ski suit. Before I could react to his outfit, he took off his glasses and began rubbing his eyes. "I am glad today will be a short day. I am just a little tired after being up all night with those military guys, *gospering* and playing cards. I am trying to learn the game they call poker, so I will be ready for Las Vegas."

His face looked pale and drawn, but his getup stole the show. I had to struggle to come up with a suitable remark: "Quite an outfit, Majid."

"Yes, this is my official guide suit. A client gave it to me. Some have called me, the Pink Panther."

"The Pink Panther is a movie star," I said.

"Oh?" He paused, seemingly stumped.

"I also am a movie star," he said.

Now, I was stumped.

"Yes, I have been in a film about the Younghusband Expedition. I was the one they called "Extra." We spent twenty-six days with two U.S. producers and a Russian film crew. They even brought make-up *womens* who worked on us. They all came to Pakistan and organized the men of Hunza. I loved being a movie star!"

"Where can I see the film, Majid?" I asked.

"I cannot truthfully say. Due to over-expense, a case has been charged against the director. But I do not know the true story—I have been *contracting* these guys with no reply. Maybe the movie will come in the theater—please watch for it. And today, you must also watch for gemstones on the ground," Majid continued. "We call this place the Shopping Mall because here we have many gemstones, like emeralds and rubies. In Pakistan, we have so many garnets, they were used to make bullets to fight against the British."

As soon as we began walking, almost every stone we passed required close examination—rocks with striations of emerald green, ruby red, and lapis blue were everywhere. Even Majid couldn't resist. Darting back and forth, we compared and wowed over our finds. Eventually, the accumulated weight put an end to our gathering, forcing us to be more selective and to discard old discoveries for new. This took even more time as we re-evaluated each other's castoffs for possible inclusion in our own caches.

After passing through rows of angular ice formations, jutting like shark fins from the glacier, the panorama opened to an amphitheater of staggering proportion. Nine days after starting out, we had reached Concordia, at elevation fifteen thousand feet, the junction of the Baltoro and Goodwin-Austen Glaciers. From Concordia, we had a 360-degree view of eight thousand meter peaks (mountains higher than twenty-six-thousand feet).

*Angular ice formations jut upward from the surface of the Baltoro Glacier.*

"May I *attention* you! Here we have K2, the second highest mountain in the world," Majid boomed, his arms outstretched.

At the end of a corridor, framed by some of the world's tallest peaks, stood K2. We had arrived in perfect weather to a place so amazing, the question "Why?" seemed self evident. I paused to gaze, not wanting the moment to end. To my astonishment, Majid took my hand and reeled me around in a mock waltz. We glided and spun to an imaginary beat—the Pink Panther and an American woman—dancing blissfully on ice, while our porters cheered and laughed.

*K2 (28,251') viewed from Concordia*

The Balti people call K2 *Chogori,* Great Mountain. So why K2? K2 is a geologic designation—a reference point assigned by British surveyors to the second mountain in the Karakoram they measured.

We spent the afternoon taking in sights as impressive as they were beautiful: Broad Peak, Gasherbrum IV, and Marble Peak were all within walking distance. By evening, clouds had gathered on the horizon, and as the sun dropped lower in the sky, magical beams of amber and rose set the mountains aglow in a light show like no other. I chased pictures with my camera, knowing my shots could never do justice to reality.

*Broad Peak (26,401') at sunset*

*Gasherbrum (26,360') at sunset, viewed from Concordia*

*Marble Peak (20,523') viewed from Concordia with K2 visible in background*

*K2 at sunset*

I found a boulder and sat alone, content to be insignificant amidst such grandeur, and watched K2's triangular silhouette meld into the approaching night sky. There was something very right about K2 being out there. If it weren't, our world would be a lesser place.

When I awoke in the morning, my tent felt damp and had sagged in so close to my face, my breath had formed a glittering glaze of frozen condensation on the fabric. Through the dim light, I saw shadows of snow piled up high against the tent walls. I knew Majid and Ismail had slept in the cook tent, but I worried about our porters. They had slept crammed together in open rock enclosures, just two feet high, with only their plastic tarp for protection.

Outside, I could barely see ten feet through the thick air. Dense fog and driving snow had reduced visibility to a gloomy, claustrophobic lead gray—K2 had vanished altogether. *Good thing we arrived yesterday, or all our effort would have been for nothing*, I thought. Standing in two feet of wet snow, I first cleared my tent of soggy mush, and then took refuge inside the cook tent, where Majid and Ismail were already hard at work. By the end of our rushed breakfast, the weather had deteriorated further. "We must leave now. If we become trapped here, we will run out of food," Majid said.

This place, so magical the night before, had turned into a nebulous maze of intimidating ice ridges. Flat light distorted perception, making features difficult to read. We chose a line down the middle of the glacier to steer clear of steep slopes, where snow was accumulating at an unsafe rate. Even worse, this new snow seemed waterlogged, making it heavier and more likely to avalanche. On the glacier's surface, flowing water had left swaths of ice-coated rock; in other places, water had undercut the ice, leaving thin overhangs, which collapsed when we stepped on them.

*Looming ice ridges near Concordia*

*A porter stands on an ice overhang where flowing water has carved a canyon into the glacier's surface.*

While rime frost accumulated on my clothing, my concern for our ill-equipped porters, many of whom lacked gloves, hats, or socks, also increased. And they all wore flimsy rubber shoes, some with holes. But they never complained or lost their footing. Not so in my case, despite my excellent footgear. Midway across one ice ledge my feet flew out, sending me sliding on my stomach down a gravel-impregnated frozen wall. My fingers dug in, my gloves shredded, a trail of blood followed. For a moment I stopped, held there like a fly on a wall, with nothing to grab onto, no footholds to be had. I was afraid to take a breath, let alone move.

Majid threw himself onto the ground and thrust his walking stick down toward me. "Grab on, Ruth. I can pull you!" he shouted.

I didn't budge. Moving a single muscle could set off another slide, but staying put would eventually net the same result.

"Grab on!" Majid yelled again.

I took aim and mustered my entire energy into an upward lunge. The instant I moved, my hold broke. Majid dove forward—I grabbed his walking stick, certain I would take him down with me. I was dead weight, the worst kind. I kept my eyes focused on his red face as he managed a hand-over-hand retrieval. *How powerful trust is ... and how fragile.*

Once off the traverse, we found a level spot, free of slush and muck, where we could all sit and recover. Majid pulled out his typhoid meds and downed more pills. After a long silence, he spoke. "It is good we left when we did. By now, there must be a meter of new snow at Concordia." Pulling a package of cookies from his pack, he passed them around. "This will be our lunch today. We must conserve food in case the weather worsens."

"How are you feeling, Majid?" I asked.

"I am feeling stronger now," he replied.

*Moving down to a lower altitude will wear less on his body,* I thought. By now, the fog had begun to lift, affording a disturbing view. Swirls of cloud obscured everything except a few jagged peaks. Ethereal contours of vapor rose and descended, echoing the topography in cloud canyons and peaks and casting shadows on the glacier below. Above us, high winds stripped snow from ridges, exposing cornices of ice that looked like enormous waves cresting over sea walls, poised to crash. This was anything but a healing place.

*Karakoram peaks shrouded in clouds*

For some reason, Majid returned to the subject of politics. "Pakistan would be better if it reunited with India. When the British split us from India in 1947, families were separated. Some family members were cut off in India, others in Pakistan. We are all supposed to be enemies, which is very hard on some families. And now, we have these extremist guys trying to get their way. The terrorism in Pakistan is like mafia families with threats aimed at chiefs of different factions, not so much at outsiders. When one guy gets killed, there is a revenge murder."

Exactly my concern—catching a stray bullet intended for someone else. This is why I was happy out on the glacier—with only earthquakes, crevasses, rockslides, and avalanches to worry about. But in this weather, a hasty retreat was the right call.

By the time we'd dropped to fourteen thousand feet, the falling snow had turned to sleet, and rising temperatures were making conditions even less stable. In the distance, a billowing cloud of snow rose up from where an avalanche had just hit. Not until several seconds later did the sound—like a sonic boom—reach us.

I kept eyeing a glacier hanging from a high ridge where ice repeatedly broke off, falling down the same path. This very avalanche chute led precisely to our campsite. Because we were required by law to camp here, we couldn't just pick another campsite at random. Only a shallow gully, already overflowing with fallen ice, separated us from the slide path. Perched at the brink of the gully sat my tent, which our porters had erected away from the others, with my privacy in mind. *Surely they know from experience this spot is safe,* I told myself, as I studied the site.

Then, in the dead of night—*avalanche.* The force shook the ground. I bolted upright, disoriented, and tried to run, not easy from within a tent and sleeping bag. There were so many zippers between me and escape—my sleeping bag zipper, tent door, and pants zipper—none of which worked in a rush. I didn't want to end up outside, bare-legged; on the other hand, propriety under these circumstances was going to kill me. I was almost through the door, when another avalanche hit close by, this time sending boulders and blocks of ice bouncing by either side of my tent. I listened until the last of them had rolled to a halt, then allowed myself to exhale. I had just failed the avalanche drill.

Still inside my tent, I stared into darkness and flopped back down, relieved to have survived a crisis. But, CRASH! This time, ice free-fell, with no warning before it hit. Again, my timing was too late. I glanced at my watch—4:15 in the morning. Distracted and exhausted, I wondered if people who live in denial really do live longer.

Another rumble. Enough! I crawled from my tent and maneuvered through boulder-and-ice-strewn darkness to the cook tent, where our entire crew huddled together after a sleepless night. Majid had already packed. No breakfast today—this battleground of nature was no place to linger and dine.

Throughout the day, we heard more avalanches—one sounding like a 747 jumbo jet landing. Along the way, Majid hurried me past a place where another group had once stopped for a rest break, recalling that six minutes after they'd resumed walking, an avalanche had wiped out the spot where they'd been sitting.

By the time we'd dropped another thousand feet, it was raining. We were at thirteen thousand feet—more advantageous than fifteen thousand feet, where over a meter of new snow had likely fallen.

Reaching our campsite, we settled into our tents, wondering what this night would bring.

In pitch blackness, I awoke to what sounded like a landslide, followed by a rush of water, very close by. Going outside to investigate, I discovered a new river channel flowing only inches from where I was camped. It had happened so suddenly—first nothing, now this. I rushed to dig a trench around the perimeter of my tent. As long as another tributary didn't add to this flow, I'd be safe from flooding, I told myself. I hadn't counted on drowning inside my own tent.

"The weather is breaking up. We must move!" Majid shouted, before the sun had risen. We quickly packed our gear and started climbing up a mountainside, taking a detour around an impassible section of glacier. In the predawn light, the mountain peaks appeared suspended on a mantle of cloud. Rooster tails of new snow rode updrafts aloft, while avalanches roared down slopes, at times crashing into slower slides below them. On a ridgeline, a solitary ibex stood with intrepid grace, its long neck and rack silhouetted against the morning sky.

*The Great Trango Tower as clouds begin to lift*

Our mountain detour dropped in a steep path as it led back to the Baltoro Glacier, ending abruptly at two boulders the size of small houses. Scrambling around them, Majid said, "The old trail runs under these two rocks. They fell here three months ago." Anxious to get clear of this slide-prone area, we climbed back onto the glacier, which by now had collapsed in many places. Grateful for every bit of boot tread, yet still slipping and sliding over rocks and ice, I skirted crevasses, straddled crevasses, and nearly fell into crevasses for the better part of the day. Each time I had to leap over another, I knew if I misjudged the distance or a lip collapsed, no one could come to my rescue. Jumping across one final crevasse, we scrambled off the ice and back onto solid ground. I paused for a final look at the Karakoram, its spires phantomlike through the mist.

To leave the glacier was to return to life: Paiyu, which had seemed so stark when we first camped there, now looked like a garden paradise. When we reached Paiyu, some of our porters were already preparing to leave. "We will not need these men anymore, so I will send them home," Majid explained. "Before they leave, you can give *baksheesh* to them. It is one of our more colorful traditions." I already knew this Urdu word could mean either *tip* or *bribe*.

"It is customary to pay each porter one hundred rupees," Majid continued.

"But Majid, they deserve more!" I insisted. With an exchange rate of fifty rupees to our dollar, we were talking only two dollars per man for the entire trip, which seemed unthinkable.

"No, Ruth. They will be unhappy in the future if others do not pay as well. This is our way, please. The porters are waiting."

Majid conducted a little going-away ceremony. After carefully folding all the rupees into neat stacks, he asked the porters to form a line, and with great deliberation presented each man his allotment. I stood at Majid's side as our departing friends filed past and thanked each one. It offered me little comfort that I'd given high-quality sunglasses to all of them at the beginning of our trip.

The sun was already burning with laser-like intensity when we set out in the morning, following the Braldu River downstream. By now, with winter fast approaching, upper-elevation temperatures had dropped, slowing the melting of ice and reducing the river to three shallow branches. "We can go through the water this time," Majid said. "It will be easier than climbing around."

Like school boys playing hooky at a local swimming hole, our porters eagerly abandoned the traditional cover-up policy and rolled their pants up to their thighs. Not me; I remained fully clothed. Majid and Ismail anchored a rope while two porters grabbed the other end and dashed into the river. The rushing water knocked them off balance, but they muscled their way across, making slow progress against the current. The line went taut—the second porter disappeared underwater. He surfaced, wide-eyed but smiling, and fought his way to the far bank. There, both porters huddled together and caught their breath while everyone else hooted and hollered.

With the rope manned on either end, porters began crossing one at a time, their backs fully loaded, using only the rope for support. I noted the effort it took each man to reach the opposite side. Once across, they dropped their loads and lent a hand to the anchor team.

My turn. The glacial water boiled up chest deep, creating an unsettling feeling of buoyancy. The cold stopped my breath and sapped my strength—my legs ached. Probing with my feet, rocks shifted too easily, throwing me off balance. The current, stronger than I had expected, tore at my clothing and pack, adding to the drag as water ripped past. I clutched the line, eager to get across. Once back on land, I was glad it took only moments for the sun to warm me up.

Their task completed, the anchor team leapt into the river and splashed toward us. With everyone safe, the pageant of legs ended. We loaded up and covered roughly fifteen miles, kicking dust as we continued downstream toward Ascolie, the village where we had begun our trek.

We spent the next day travelling through the Bombing Range. Judging by the amount of newly fallen rock, it had been acting up in our absence. Several days later, we came trudging in off the hot trail near the outskirts of Ascolie, where a sign leaning against a lonely dirt hovel advertised, COKES FOR SALE, 100 RUPEES. I bought a round for everyone. But when we tried to pry off the caps, we discovered they had rusted onto the bottles. Disappointed, we returned the Cokes to the vendor and left—he rueing lost profit, and we still thirsty.

Not long afterward, our Coke salesman caught up to us with fresh inventory. Unable to resist, I again bought a round for everyone. When Majid tried to force the cap off of his bottle, the neck shattered in his hand. In a well-intended salvage effort, Ismail poured the contents of the broken bottle through a wire mesh, which didn't look fine enough for the job. Proud of his quick thinking, he presented a cup of filtered Coke to Majid. Before I could stop him, Majid had downed the Coke.

For the next few hours I kept an eye on Majid, all the while agonizing over what to do if he took a turn for the worse. Nothing happened.

As soon as we showed up in Ascolie, the place came alive. Locals hustled about in an air of excitement, throwing open doors to display a variety of odds and ends, ranging from goatskin boots to tourmaline crystals. Within moments, the settlement transformed into a mini-mall as huts became shops. The bolder villagers rushed me with their goods in an effort to beat out the competition, their neighbors. When I tried to escape to our cook tent, they moved their inventory to just outside the door. "Madam, special for you: best final price!" they would taunt.

While I dodged hawkers, our porters spruced up for their return home, trimming hair and beards and switching to their city clothes. Majid again collected baksheesh for the going-away ceremony. Before they dispersed, our oldest porter, named Hassan, approached me. Bowing, he took a loop of twine from his own neck and tied it around mine. From the twine hung a stone pendant shaped in the crescent-and-star symbol of Islam.

Majid translated: "Ruth, Hassan has carved this for you from medicine stone. He says it has a purpose: if you feel depressed, grind it against a rock and put the powder in water to drink. It will make you fine again." Overhearing, the other porters gathered around to examine and admire Hassan's work. Majid further honored Hassan by asking if he could make a pendant for his wife, too. Judging by his expression, Hassan seemed pleased. To thank Hassan, I only needed to take his hand and squeeze it. He knew that meant a genuine thank-you. With a squeeze of the hand, we parted.

We heard the distant backfire of an engine long before the vehicle came into sight. Then, a cross between a jeep and a small pickup truck pulled into camp. Mounted on the front end was an ibex head, "for good luck," according to Majid. Eight porters scrambled onboard, standing, balancing, and hanging onto whatever they could find. Waving good-bye through a belch of exhaust, I stood in the road watching until they were gone. *These endings always feel so empty: you walk with people as journey partners, then leave them forever. But I promised to send photos, and I will,* I thought.

"Another jeep will come for us soon," Majid muttered, as he oversaw the final pack-up of our camp.

Another jeep did not come—not that day, anyway. We unpacked and set up camp once more. By morning, we had all but exhausted our food and were down to a Pakistani version of corn flakes. Standing outside the cook tent munching mindlessly on cereal, I watched Ismail repack the kitchen "for the last time," according to Majid.

The jeep-and-wagon rig—the one with the ibex head—ultimately returned around noon. It would carry us back to Skardu and all the way to Hunza. Eleven of us jumped onboard. Find a place or be left behind: we had three people up front, six standing in the open-air back, and two riding shotgun with only their toes resting on the rear bumper. Clinging to the nearest handhold—often each other—we set out on the white-knuckle drive back to civilization, careening along with the rig's rear bumper almost touching the ground. For shock absorption, standing, I quickly discovered, proved preferable to sitting on the metal toolbox.

Midway up Inshallah Pass, on one of many three-point curves (forward-back, forward-back, forward-and-back again), our engine stalled and died. Frantically, our driver tried the starter—nothing. The jeep began rolling backward, accelerating downhill—the two porters riding on the rear bumper dove off in terror. In a last-ditch effort, the driver popped the clutch. One whiplashing lurch, and the engine kicked over. We resumed creeping to the top of the pass, where we picked up the two who had bailed.

Next, the hair-raising descent into the Indus River canyon. Even after weeks in extreme surroundings, the road looked more terrifying now than it had on the trip in. To keep my balance, I hung onto the nearest available body and tried to focus on a fixed object—our ibex hood ornament—while the landscape blurred past. The ninety-mile drive took almost six hours.

Once we were clear of the river canyon, we stopped at a little Afghan restaurant alongside the road. Plastered across the front door was a poster of Ayatollah Khomeini. Inside, rugs and cushions covered the floor, and in the center of the room stood a heavy artillery shell, six feet tall—the only décor in an otherwise Spartan environment. *Great, my country bombs Afghanistan, and I drop in for a friendly little lunch.*

Majid quickly ushered me to a quiet corner of the room where we took our places on pillows. Meanwhile, the other customers (all male) glared. I adjusted my veil, once again grateful to have it, and hoped my respectful appearance would help. Only Majid spoke, ordering our meal from the stone-faced proprietor who clearly did not appreciate our business—he practically threw plates of food at us. "These are not people I know. In Hunza it will be different," whispered Majid.

Once we were back in our jeep, Majid relaxed and resumed his role as tour guide. "This drive to Hunza used to take nineteen hours, but now it only takes six. This is a new road through valleys and tribes, each with a unique dialect and culture. These areas were once completely forgotten—people had to walk many days for essentials, and the sick died for lack of medical treatment. They had no radios, TVs, or cars. But now they are connected with today's world."

The bridge spanning the Indus River looked to be two hundred yards across. Just short of the bridge, a soldier signaled us to stop. Majid and our driver followed him into a guardhouse, returning ten minutes later. The wooden crossbeams groaned and rattled as we rolled onto the bridge, which was barely wide enough for one vehicle.

Halfway across, the guard on the other side ran toward us, waving his arms and blustering in urgent tones. Our driver objected loudly, but in the end threw the jeep into reverse. After we had backed all the way off the bridge, a great show of power erupted as the two guards met midway, shouting at each other, while our driver yelled at them both. For thirty minutes, we waited and watched as the three men pointed fingers at each other and at us. In the end, we were granted permission to cross. The six-hour drive to Hunza took nine.

# II.

# AN AFTERNOON *EXCRETION*

*Adventure is when you can't dial 911, and even if you could, no one would come.*

Apple, apricot, walnut, and mulberry trees lined the road to Karimabad, the capital of Hunza. Set in a valley at eight thousand feet high, Karimabad once served as an important center of slave trade and a stopping point for camel caravans. At the entrance to Karimabad, the rock spires of Rakaposhi rose to over twenty-five-thousand feet. High on the opposite mountainside, against a backdrop of ice-clad cliffs and peaks, stood the six-hundred-year-old Baltit Fort. Supported by wood beams to protect against earthquakes—some of the world's largest—this fortress once housed the Mirs, the former rulers of Hunza. "The last Mir was ousted in 1974 when Hunza became part of Pakistan," Majid said. "He married a dancer from Lahore. This was considered quite scandalous."

*The Baltit Fort in Hunza*

Karimabad itself looked like a hanging garden sandwiched between two massive gorges, where glacial water free-fell to the valley below. Flat-roofed homes of mud and timbers, each with meandering rock-walled terraces, stair-stepped up the mountainsides. Below, the Hunza River cut a cleft over one thousand feet deep through the valley floor, which was otherwise covered in cultivated fields. Lining either side of the road were hedgerows of marijuana plants, five feet tall. Children played hide-and-seek in them, while cows browsed on the leaves. Coincidently, they did sell Laughing Cow cheese in Hunza.

"Locals in Hunza do not smoke the marijuana leaves. We chew the seeds for good health and to make the body strong," Majid said. He had the driver stop while he picked three seeds. I tried one—it tasted like popcorn. He continued, "When Westerners used to come here, they smoked the marijuana leaves. Those guys were what we call 'happy tourists,' which is to say, they came here to buy and deal drugs. We could always tell who they were. These types always looked like they had been away from home a long time. They were here to smuggle drugs out of our country."

As I soon learned, the men of Hunza preferred their own vices. They drank a rotgut concoction called *Hunza water*. Home-brewed from mulberries, this clear alcoholic drink could be carried around in ordinary mineral water bottles without anyone suspecting. But taking a sip was always a dead giveaway, as eyes watered up and faces turned bright red. Smoking cigarettes also seemed popular, except around elders.

"Some say Hunza is the ancient Shangri-La, and we are descendants of soldiers lost from Alexander the Great's army when he invaded India. This is why our coloring is so different from those in Punjab, to the south, where they look more like people from India. Even our local dialect is unrelated to any other language known. Hunza is unique for having people who live beyond the age of one hundred. We believe this may be due to minerals in our glacial water," Majid said.

This purported longevity might also be attributed to the high concentration of laetrile in apricot pits, eaten in Hunza as a staple, so I had read. But as I later learned, apricot pits also contain high concentrations of strychnine—*the pits*, so to speak. Still, locals told of old men "on their third set of teeth." But birth records seemed scarce in Hunza. Majid thought he might be "twenty-eight, or maybe thirty-three." His mother was "fifty or sixty." He didn't know his father's age and said these matters were not important to the people of Hunza.

"Less than one percent of the people of Pakistan live in the north," Majid continued. "In Hunza, we measure population by the number of houses—six hundred, with eleven family members per house. The only way a person can receive land is through inheritance. Here we say, to sell our land is to sell our children."

On our way to a guest house owned by Majid's *family*, we drove through a tiny business district where bored-looking merchants sat outside their shops. "Because there are no tourists, business has been very difficult. You will be safe here," Majid said. After checking in, I wandered onto the street and strolled up the hill. The town appeared deserted, except for a few shopkeepers. One proprietor, leaning against a wall, had dozed off and was about to fall over. Catching himself just in time, he snapped to and gently beckoned me to consider his wares of woven rugs, donkey bags, and gemstones of various qualities.

"So you are American," a voice from within another shadowy shop said. "Americans usually pretend to be Canadians when they are in Pakistan, but we can always tell by their accent. It has been very dangerous for Americans here. I tell them, 'Get out! Get on a plane and fly to Islamabad. Leave the country.'"

This unsolicited information came across as a veiled threat. I turned to escape, but the voice continued: "I am Majid's cousin. I saw you arrive with him. Please, come in."

I paused, then stepped inside and examined a small flute, while he made polite conversation. After buying the flute, I slipped away to the Mir Hotel for lunch, where I felt uncomfortably conspicuous sitting alone in the empty dining room. Eventually a waiter appeared and handed me a menu. To my surprise it featured *Mir Burgers*.

"I'll have a hamburger, please," I said to my waiter.

"Oh no, madam, we do not have hamburgers," he answered.

"What's this *Mir Burger*?" I asked.

"It is a beef burger, madam," he responded.

*Of course it's a beef burger. In this Muslim culture they don't eat ham-anything—they don't touch pork.*

"Perfect! I'll have the *Mir Burger*, please," I said.

Secession to the Mir's throne occurred when the Mir's oldest son killed Dad, usually with a sword. I wondered just how long ago this practice had been abolished. My *Mir Burger* was served.

Back at my guesthouse another newspaper headline caught my eye: TALIBAN ESCALATE AS AFGHAN TROOPS MOBILIZE FOR HOLY WAR. Just as being out on the Baltoro Glacier, nothing here was certain.

The following morning Majid announced a "special *excretion*" for the day. Majid's English was great and greatly appreciated by me, especially when compared to my Urdu, but I couldn't help enjoying the occasional slip. Our excursion would take us up the Khunjerab Pass, via the Karakoram Highway (KKH for short), topping out at an altitude of 16,200 feet. I clambered into the jeep already knowing my place, the backseat. While we bounced down the road, our driver echoed what I'd heard from shop owners: "During recent months, Americans have not been safe here."

His warning might just as well have applied to jeep travel. Calling the KKH a highway was a stretch—it was a narrow ribbon, paved in places, cut into the mountainside, and no wider than my driveway at home. On one side of the highway, rock walls shot straight up; off the other side, a cliff dropped thousands of feet to the Indus

River. According to Majid, at least one vehicle every month plunged from the KKH into the raging Indus.

*Why does he always tell me these things?* I asked myself.

The few villages we saw looked like tiny garden oases set into an otherwise chaotic landscape. Our driver navigated at a snail's pace through one goat herd after another, sometimes coming to a complete stop and turning off the engine to let them pass. These goats created problems by scouring slopes of vegetation and kicking rocks loose, which set off landslides, he complained. As we entered the immense Indus River canyon, we had a bird's eye view from the aptly named Sky Bridge. "The Chinese built this bridge for us as part of the Frontier Works Organization, founded through joint agreement between China and Pakistan," Majid explained.

"We have come to the border," Majid declared, as we pulled up to a gate flying two flags, Pakistan's and China's. "Please, I need your passport now." As soon as Majid entered the guardhouse, a covey of chukar partridge darted out from nearby brush to forage alongside our jeep. Soon, a guard opened the gate and ushered us into Khunjerab National Park, home to Marco Polo sheep, ibex, snow leopard, Tibetan wolf, and Himalayan snow cock, to mention a few.

As the grade increased, the road deteriorated. Where mountainside had been blasted away to create roadbed, sharp rock slabs overhung the highway, guillotine-like. "Workers had to be lowered down mountainsides on ropes to drill holes in these walls for explosives," Majid said, beginning his recitation. "During sixteen years of construction, more than five hundred Chinese and Pakistani workers lost their lives, with one life sacrificed for each kilometer."

*Why did this not surprise me?*

By now, all signs of life had vanished, and the weather had closed in. I noticed my seatbelt was secured to the jeep's frame with a safety pin. The jeep pushed on.

It began to snow. The windshield wipers didn't work—neither did the car heater. The rear windows had curtains, but no glass, so snow began blowing in and accumulating on my Pakistani dress. Only five hours out and already we were at sixteen thousand feet—higher than we had been at Concordia after weeks of hiking. Majid pointed out a faint path, barely visible along the slope above us, and said it was part of the original Silk Route, traveled by Marco Polo on his journey east.

*Marco should have stayed at home…*

It started snowing harder. Just short of the summit, our jeep engine began making unusual noises—metal-on-metal—like a roller coaster being cranked up the highest hill. Majid and our driver discussed the situation in low, serious tones—in Urdu. I didn't need to understand the language to catch the gist—the frequent *Inshallahs* conveyed enough. Then, the inevitable occurred: the jeep quit altogether.

*The vehicular breakdown—not if, but when, how often, and where along the cliff you are when it happens.*

Our driver jumped out first and lifted the hood—Majid and I got out, too, and looked on. We all stared at the engine—stared at each other—stared at the engine again. In a futile attempt to stay warm, I climbed back inside the jeep, while Majid and our driver argued like politicians. Finally our driver poked his head inside and announced, "I now know the problem with the engine, madam. I have isolated the problem. A part is broken!"

Nearby, two bored Pakistani soldiers watched all this from their guardhouse, a solitary one-room rock hut. Knowing, no doubt from experience, our predicament would take time to resolve (if at all), they came over and invited me inside for tea.

"Do not worry. The director of Khunjerab Park is from my *family*," Majid said. "I will send word down to headquarters requesting another vehicle. It will be here soon."

"Soon" dragged out to hours as I sat on a cot by a rusty kerosene stove and sipped tea. Eventually, Majid appeared with another announcement: "I have new information. The jeep has one gear that works. Reverse!"

He disappeared.

*I began thinking about the fall of nations, the extinction of species, namely my own. And survival—how once a certain amount has happened, you begin to wonder, what else could possibly go wrong?*

Majid returned with the New Plan: "*Inshallah,* the other vehicle will soon be on its way. We must begin coasting slowly down the pass to intercept it."

*Coasting slowly down a 16,200 foot high pass in Pakistan?*

So began "The Coast"—not in reverse—not in any gear. Now, there were new odors: the smell of burning brakes, burning rubber, burning metal. And this was only the beginning—we were at sixteen thousand feet.

*And to think we could have died on the Baltoro Glacier. But no, we saved that for the KKH.*

We sped down the road, coasting the Silk Route wide-eyed, occasionally catching glimpses of bridges so far below, they looked like tinker toys. Majid, his face white, braced his arms straight out in front of him with his hands pressed against the dashboard. Each time we swung wide on a curve, which happened on every curve, he grabbed the roof strut and looked as though he'd lapsed into a catatonic state. Fortunately, we had the road to ourselves. In fact, we hadn't seen another vehicle all day, which wasn't comforting either. I wondered, which would be worse: to have cars to hit or to be all alone out here?

DANGER OF DEATH read a crude sign, as we swerved around another curve—no further explanation needed. Now I understood why trucks in this part of the world had GOOD LUCK painted on their bumpers.

*A truck rounds a curve on the KKH.*

Majid ordered our driver to pull over: "I do not know where the other jeep is. It has been two hours since I last radioed, and we have not passed anyone."

Another jeep did come into view, but from the wrong direction. Having spotted us as it rounded the last curve, it pulled up behind. Introductions were exchanged, and quickly, all heads were under our hood. Majid filled me in: "This man is not from my family, but he is married to a woman from my family, so he is OK. He says when something inside the engine is broken, it is useless to wait—we should just keep driving until it stops. He will go behind us."

So, sticking with local knowledge, that's what we did. Our driver released the brake. We began rolling forward, instantly accelerating too fast for Majid's comfort. He ordered our driver to pull over again. Letting out a long breath, Majid jumped out to flag down our chase vehicle. After conferring briefly with the other driver, Majid reported back: "From this point on, it is flat enough for the other jeep to tow us."

*Flat?!*

The towline was set in place using what looked like old household telephone wire. "Pakistani system!" our driver assured me. A sharp jolt—the rescue vehicle moved forward with our jeep rolling only three feet behind. Majid's body went rigid as he pressed himself back into his seat to offset a possible rear-end collision. More *Inshallahs.* "The Tow" proved even more frightening than "The Coast." On each curve, we skirted so close to the cliff's edge, I could look straight down at the river, thousands of feet below. Whenever our tow line slackened, a sudden jerk followed when it yanked tight. I coined a new term, *jeeplash.*

"We are driving to Sust, the first town in Pakistan as you come over the pass from China. We will have the engine repaired there," Majid said.

*Only if we arrive in one piece, Majid.*

On the bright side, our wild ride down the mountain had saved us another very long walk. While the jeep was being repaired in Sust, Majid and our driver took off on foot to buy cigarettes and *Chinese water* (alcohol). Waiting behind gave me time to study the outrageous Pakistani trucks, grinding and squealing past the repair shop. It was as though the circus had come to town. Their cabs and trailers were covered with paintings of lions, tigers, butterflies, peacocks, monkeys, and eyeballs. Metallic fringe and beads hung from bumpers and window frames, with windshield wipers wrapped in colored foil. And their drivers were equally flamboyant: when they noticed me watching, several jockeyed for positions to better show off their rigs.

When they spotted my camera, this further fueled the dynamic already in play.

*Pakistani truck*

Ultimately, we made it back to Hunza "safely." *Day eight-hundred,* I thought, dragging myself from bed the next morning. I felt more beat-up after one day of driving than I had the entire time on the Baltoro Glacier.

"Planes can only fly if the weather is good," Majid said of our aborted flight to Islamabad. "We will go by jeep instead." Not my first choice, as I still felt woozy after the previous day's mild carsickness, and not-so-mild adrenaline rushes.

We took off south toward Gilgit, an area "once inhabited by unicorns and gold-digging ants the size of foxes," according to Majid. "Near Gilgit, we have the highest polo ground in the world, over twelve thousand-feet high. The game started here. *Polo* is the Balti word for ball. In the old days, they used a goat head for a ball."

*An afternoon polo match in Gilgit*

Driving through one dreadful town after another and passing numerous car accidents and breakdowns along the way, I thanked my lucky stars that our jeep still worked. At dusk, we pulled into a grim little commercial row, made even worse in the fading light of day. The place felt sinister. Lining either side of the road were small, dimly lit merchant stalls, displaying guns and weapons of every make, about which I knew nothing. (They didn't give the impression of being intended for sport.)

"Would you like to get out and look around?" Majid asked enthusiastically.

"No thanks, Majid. I'll just stay here in the jeep," I heard myself say. My mind had retreated to another place.

"But here we can see pen guns. You can buy them as souvenirs," Majid persisted.

"Majid, I don't need a pen gun," I responded.

But Majid had his heart set on showing me a pen gun. "I will ask this shop owner to bring one out for you to see," he insisted. Before I could object, Majid leapt from the jeep and ran to the nearest stall, returning moments later with the vendor and what appeared to be a ballpoint pen. He shoved it into my hand. The thing looked and felt evil—cold, lead-grey, much heavier than a pen, and in no way a harmless writing instrument.

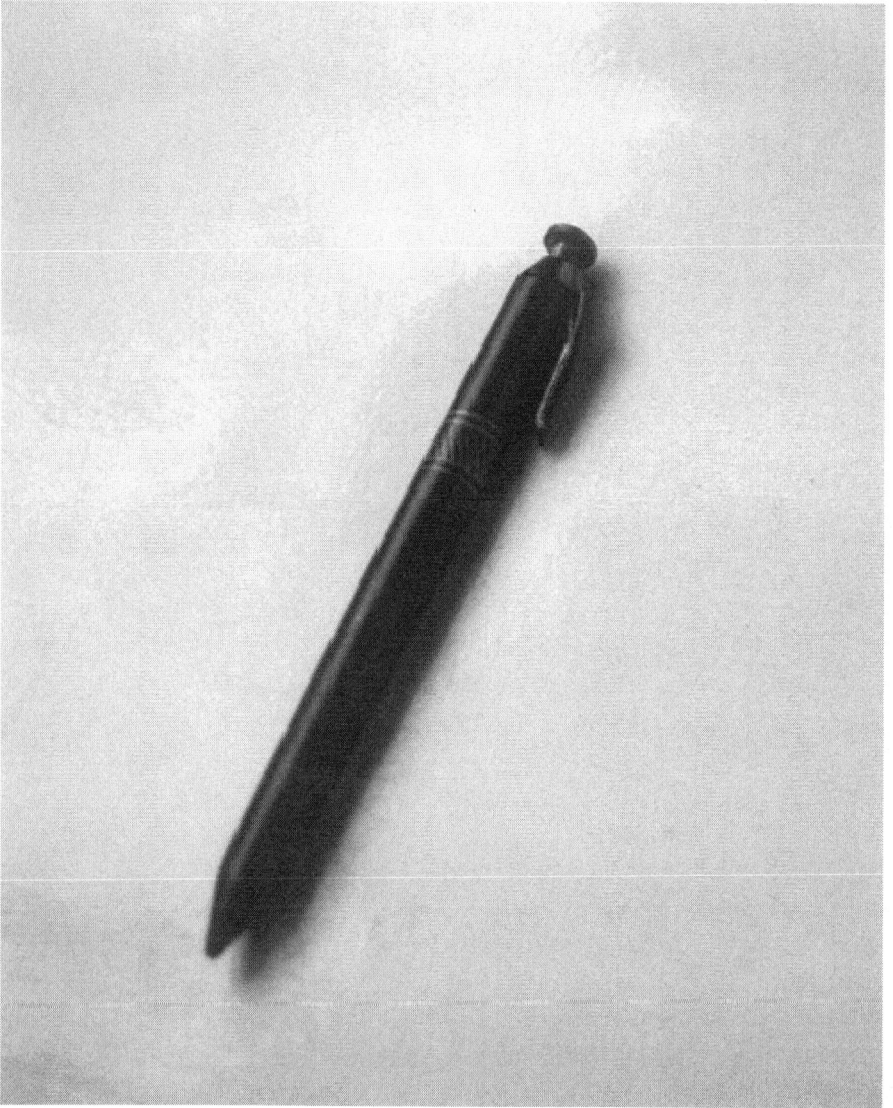

*Pen gun*

"Now, I will show you how it shoots!" Majid said.

"No, Majid, it won't be necessary," I responded.

The insidious device was like something from a James Bond movie—a small weapon resembling a ballpoint pen, except this one fired a bullet when the end was depressed. There were cigarette-lighter guns, too—pop the top and a bullet got you in the throat.

"Do you want to take one home?" Majid asked.

"No thanks, Majid," I replied.

*Terrific ... our embassy has evacuated, Americans are targets here, Pakistan is at war with India, and Majid wants me to smuggle a weapon out of the country.*

Majid sent the disappointed vendor back to his stall as our driver started up our engine. Darkness had fallen by the time we reached our hotel—which wouldn't make it to most people's list—a walled government complex, set along the Indus River, where we were the only guests. In the lobby, I found a newspaper with headlines about Iran and Pakistan pulling their embassy staffs from each other's country. But for now, my concerns were more immediate: it was eleven at night, tomorrow we'd drive to Islamabad, and it was raining—raining hard.

In the morning, we continued our drive south toward Islamabad. As we left the foothills, the terrain leveled out and temperatures soared. A thick layer of haze hung above fields of mustard and rice. But my mind focused on one thing—reaching the city.

Back in Islamabad we met up with Ziad, on the mend and chipper, having successfully dodged a return to K2 with me. To make up for his absence on the trek, he offered to take me to Taxilla, just outside Islamabad, the center of a once-powerful Buddhist empire during the Gandhara Period (500 to 600 AD).

In route, we stopped at a local restaurant for lunch. When Ziad and I sat down together at a table, the manager rushed over: "Oh no, madam, you cannot sit here. You must sit there." He pointed me to a small table against the far wall, enclosed in heavy floor-to-ceiling curtains. There, I ate lunch, alone. After we left the restaurant, Ziad apologized. But I was unruffled. I had come to Pakistan to experience the culture, not to challenge it.

Later in the afternoon, we checked in with the Minister of Expeditions. To my surprise, he seemed relieved to see us. I asked to return the following year to trek along a tribal belt in the Northwest Frontier Province. Specifically, I requested permission to trek the Pakistan border adjoining the Wakhan Corridor, the narrow strip of Afghanistan separating Pakistan from Tajikistan. He quickly agreed to issue a permit for anywhere under his jurisdiction. But he had no authority over this restricted tribal region along the Wakhan. When I returned the next year, I would have to go in person to the Office of Tribal Authorities and request access.

It was before dawn when Majid arrived to take me to the airport for my flight home. When we entered the airport departure hall, Majid became unusually formal, as though a wall had gone up between us. I dismissed this as the pressure he must have felt by being seen in public with a Western woman. After an awkward farewell, I joined the crowd funneling toward the security gate.

Hours later, my plane still sat on the sweltering tarmac with an instrument problem, according to the captain. Once we finally lifted off and reached cruising altitude, the captain's voice again sounded over the loud speaker: "We will be flying over Afghanistan for the next two hours at an altitude of thirty thousand feet." As I gazed out the window, the mountains appeared to be almost at eye-level. *Sadly, I thought, this may be the closest I'll ever come to Afghanistan.*

# U.S. DEPARTMENT OF STATE TRAVEL WARNING

## AUGUST 1999

*The Department of State warns U.S. citizens to evaluate carefully implications for their safety before deciding to travel to Pakistan. Osama bin Laden, indicted in the U.S. for involvement in the East-African Embassy bombings, has issued public statements threatening Americans and others. Considerable public sympathy and overt support for him exist both in Pakistan and Afghanistan.*

*Travel in the Northwest Frontier Province: Because of dangerous security conditions, caution is essential when traveling overland through tribal areas. Substantial areas within the Northwest Frontier are designated tribal areas and are outside the jurisdiction of government law-enforcement authorities. Travel within these areas is particularly hazardous. Visitors risk being caught in armed clashes between feudal tribal factions or smugglers. Abduction of foreigners is occasionally reported from tribal areas. If visitors must enter tribal areas, a permit from the Tribal Affairs Department is required. The permit may stipulate that an armed escort must accompany the visitor. Even in settled areas of the Northwest Frontier Province, ethnic, political, or sectarian violence may target foreigners.*

*MAPS ARE APPROXIMATE

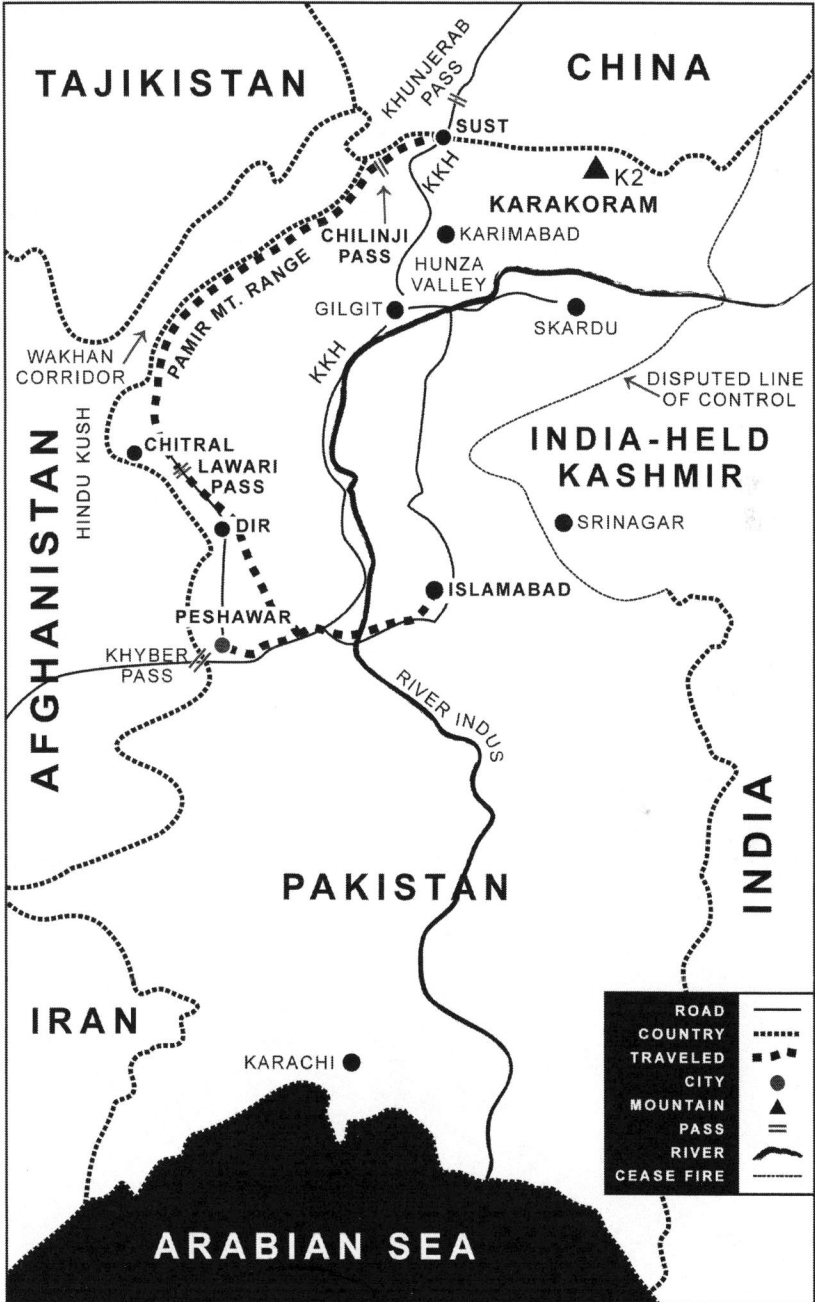

TAJIKISTAN

CHINA

KHUNJERAB PASS

SUST

KKH

▲ K2

KARAKORAM

CHILINJI PASS

KARIMABAD

HUNZA VALLEY

PAMIR MT. RANGE

GILGIT

SKARDU

KKH

WAKHAN CORRIDOR

HINDU KUSH

DISPUTED LINE OF CONTROL

INDIA-HELD KASHMIR

CHITRAL

LAWARI PASS

DIR

SRINAGAR

PESHAWAR

ISLAMABAD

KHYBER PASS

AFGHANISTAN

RIVER INDUS

INDIA

PAKISTAN

IRAN

KARACHI

ROAD
COUNTRY
TRAVELED
CITY
MOUNTAIN
PASS
RIVER
CEASE FIRE

ARABIAN SEA

*SOME OF THE BORDERS SHOWN ON THIS MAP ARE DISPUTED.

*Route traveled through the tribal belt along the Wakhan Corridor*

# III.

# STILL NOT SAFE

## Islamabad, Pakistan

### September 1999

When I returned to Islamabad for my second visit, a healthy Majid met me at the airport. The minute I spotted him, his arms opened to greet me. Laughing and catching up, we paused only while Majid hired a porter to carry my trekking bags to a waiting car. As our driver puzzled over how to stuff my duffels into his small vehicle, Majid pulled me aside.

"Ruth, why are you wearing a black veil?" he quietly asked.

"It's smaller than my other veil and easier to manage when I'm on the move," I answered.

Majid nodded understandingly and politely explained, "In Pakistan, to wear a black veil means you are in mourning for someone who has just died."

*Dressed for a funeral in Pakistan. No wonder people in the airport were so nice to me—they thought I'd flown halfway around the world for a funeral, hopefully not my own.*

"And it is better to not wear your pants so high," Majid quietly added. "In our culture, it is considered indecent to show the ankles."

I looked down. Sure enough, I could see my ankles and several inches of leg. The one-size-fits-all pants of my Pakistani ensemble were too short. "I guess they shrank when I washed them, Majid."

"Please, loosen the drawstring. Then they will hang lower," Majid said.

*Now, a floozy dressed for a funeral in Pakistan—I couldn't believe I was still bungling my way through their culture.*

Majid took me directly to my hotel and checked me in for the night. Before I went to bed, I made the suggested adjustments to my local attire. I already stood out here. I didn't need to stand out for the wrong reasons.

Jet lagged, I awoke long before the hotel dining room opened for breakfast. And I was hungry. Checking the mini-bar, I only found a prayer rug and a copy of the *Koran,* the sacred text of Islam. So I phoned the front desk and ordered coffee in my room to tide me over. Soon, a knock sounded at the door. I opened it to a boy who didn't look old enough to shave. He entered with his loaded tray. Saying thank you, I gave him a small tip. He grabbed my arm and wouldn't let go.

"Madam, I want to French kiss you," he gushed.

"No, you must leave now!" Yanking my arm free, I showed him out.

A few minutes elapsed before I heard another knock at the door. When I opened it, there stood the same boy. He pulled a ten-rupee note from his wallet, shoved it into my hand and lunged forward in an attempted embrace. I slammed the door in his face.

Later at breakfast, he showed up again, this time in the dining room. Slinking up to my table, he came up with a new ploy: "Madam, I am a student. I want to go to the United States to study."

Just then, Majid arrived and joined me. When the boy saw my local guide, he disappeared for good.

"I must apologize," Majid began. I thought he was referring to the boy. "I have not spoken English since last year. You are my first this season," he continued.

"I haven't spoken Urdu either, so you're safe," I responded. "Don't worry, we'll figure things out together."

Majid launched into his briefing. "Ruth, it is far more dangerous for Americans this year than last. There are two reasons. First, the war between India and Pakistan has now escalated as far south as Skardu. This war peaked in May with the loss of seventy-five Pakistani commissioned officers. I am sad to say, most were men from Hunza and the northern territories. Second, Osama bin Laden is at large, with the American CIA after him. Locals say he is hiding in the town of Peshawar."

"Isn't Peshawar where we go tomorrow?" I asked.

"Yes, but we will only stay one night there," Majid said, as though only one night made it OK.

"Would you like to visit the Faisal Mosque today?" he asked, changing subjects. "I think it may be possible to take you inside."

"I thought women aren't allowed in the mosque," I replied, taken back by his offer.

"They have made a special door for *womens*," Majid said, summoning our driver.

*Faisal Mosque in Islamabad*

The futuristic Faisal Mosque, a gift from King Faisal of Saudi Arabia when Pakistan relocated its capital from Karachi to Islamabad, could accommodate one hundred thousand worshippers inside and another million worshippers on the surrounding grounds, according to Majid. We crossed through manicured gardens and climbed marble steps to an expansive esplanade surrounding the entire building. In front, an impressive array of fountains shot plumes of water nearly two stories into the air. We meandered around the structure, passing under archways and across open-air verandas, each with tiered water features. "You may enter there, Ruth," Majid said, pointing toward the last door along a marble walkway. Then he disappeared into the main chamber via the men's entrance.

I removed my shoes and pulled my veil higher onto my head. The partitioned cubicle appeared to be fifteen feet square, at most. From there, I could peer through a wooden screen into the main mosque, voluminous and unadorned. Nothing happened—no service or chanting. Only a few worshippers knelt and silently prayed. An occasional padding of bare feet stirred the otherwise still air. My breathing slowed, my muscles relaxed. For a moment, time seemed to stop.

"Ismail, our cook from last year, will be joining us on the trek," Majid said when he came for me the next day. Wonderful news— Ismail was a lovely man. Soon, the three of us were off to Peshawar, gateway to the Northwest Frontier Province. Peshawar, a rough place and the center of Pakistan's black market, was known for three major industries: guns, drugs, and rugs. Peshawar sits at the base of the Khyber Pass, a lawless no-man's land under the rule of neither Pakistan nor Afghanistan. Along the Khyber Pass, vendors sold rugs, illegal drugs—hashish, marijuana, and heroin displayed openly in sales stalls—and guns of every type. For a few rupees, one could even fire a Kalashnikov or a rocket launcher "just like at an arcade," Majid said.

"This is a smuggler zone, where smugglers live in lavish mansion estates and drive expensive cars. And the one they call the Super Smuggler even has a helipad. He spends his time in London and traveling all over. They say he is the largest smuggler in the world," Majid explained.

After Majid checked us into our hotel, he led me to a table in a far corner of the dining room. There, he spoke in hushed tones: "Many people from Afghanistan are living in Peshawar now. In fact, we have a large refugee camp here. You will not see any *womens* on the street— even local *womens* do not go out, because the belief system here is so strict. I must stress again, you cannot tell people you are American."

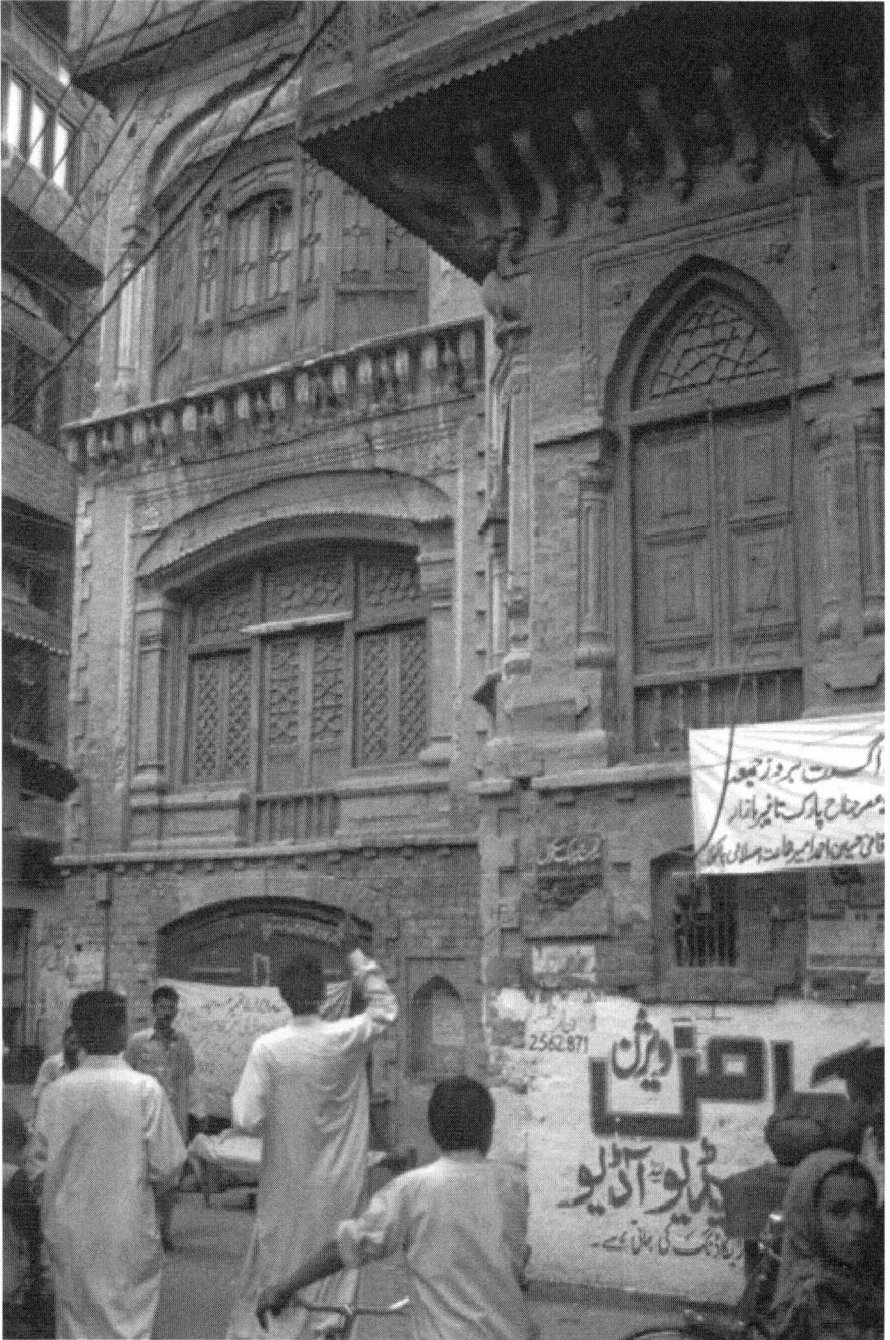

*Peshawar*

Majid walked me to my room, instructing me to stay there until he returned. This gave me time to study my new surroundings. The plaster walls looked like they'd been sprayed with machine-gun fire and the bathroom featured an oversized purple toilet seat. As I wondered if the big hook in the center of the ceiling was for a noose to hang myself, Majid knocked at the door.

"Someone in Peshawar wants to meet you," he said.

"Who?" I asked.

"A friend," Majid answered.

"What friend? I thought you didn't know anyone in Peshawar," I replied.

"It will be OK," he persisted.

Without further explanation, Majid whisked me downstairs, out the lobby, and directly across the street to a medieval building with a ponderous wooden door. The moment we reached the opposite curb, the wooden door opened. As soon as we stepped inside, one of three imposing men bolted the door shut and pulled thick tapestry curtains across it. Suddenly, I felt as though someone had sucked all the air from the room. *So this is where I disappear.*

"Where in the States are you from?" barked the oldest of the three.

I looked at Majid—Majid looked away.

"Northern Nevada," I sighed, feeling as though I'd just confessed to a felony.

"Oh, Las Vegas!" the man exclaimed.

As I tried to explain how northern Nevada is nothing like Las Vegas, he talked right over me. He had just returned from Las Vegas, where he had won so much money, he had bought his wife an $18,000 diamond ring.

"The rug business must be good here in Peshawar," I sighed.

"Indeed it is! I am the fifth generation in my family to sell carpets. Years ago, I left Afghanistan to bring the business here. Now, I sell to people all over the world. Of course, I keep the best carpets here," he said, skillfully segueing into his sales pitch.

"For example, this carpet from Iran—over 150 years old—is a family heirloom from the private collection of my own grandfather. This carpet is very close to my heart, and for this reason, I shall never sell it. But enough of this sentiment!" Without turning his head, he waved his hand back over his shoulder to a watchful attendant.

"Please, we will have green tea now." The attendant, silver tray in hand, served us. Stepping aside, he stood at attention.

Directing me to a sofa draped with silk rugs strategically placed where I couldn't avoid touching them, he positioned himself front-and-center across from me: "Now, with no obligation to you, I would like to talk about the carpets of Central Asia. Of course, this is for your information only, madam."

"Thanks, but I don't need any rugs," I said, politely shrugging him off.

It was as though I had never spoken.

Without missing a beat, he carried on, and with the grace of a maestro, orchestrated the presentation of each and every carpet. His jowls flapped; beads of sweat formed along his brow.

I sat silent, erect, arms crossed.

"I really don't need any rugs," I repeated.

Wagging his index finger from side to side, the dealer met my objection in a tone as smooth as silk: "Madam, carpets are not to need. They are to love and to treasure like gold—these days they are even better than gold!"

The more I objected, the more beautiful were the rugs presented. Finally he had me—I gasped and leaned forward, instantly drawn to a pattern of gold threads woven throughout a field of crimson.

"This carpet is very special," the dealer said, raising his finger again. The attendant stepped forward and rotated the rug 180 degrees. The entire color palate magically shifted to crimson-on-gold. "Madam, now you can see how light plays on the silk from this direction. The cut of the threads is what catches the light."

The owner searched my eyes. I focused on the rug's mesmerizing sheen.

"Perhaps you like better quality?" he suggested, lifting one corner of another rug and pointing to the back. "Note the number of knots, each hand-tied." He flipped the rug over and continued: "This is finer. You can see, yes? Please, touch it." The attendant lifted the carpet to my lap. It felt like a Persian cat.

I rubbed my brow.

"Would you like more tea, madam?" he asked, signaling again for the silver tray. "Perhaps you would like a moment to think about this," he added. The dealer slipped away; his attendant stayed. Something told me the attendant understood every word, every eye movement I made.

"So you have decided to buy them all, yes?" the dealer said, returning. "Which credit card do you prefer, madam? Of course, the price is better if you pay with cash—you have my word on this. For a small additional cost, we can ship it for you in a box. It will be very safe, I can assure you." On cue, the attendant stepped forward holding a carton for my examination and approval.

"Or we can deliver the carpet to your hotel in Islamabad, so you can carry it onto your flight home. This is a rare opportunity—there is no reason not to own a carpet of such quality. It is our duty to help, because we cannot bear to watch our customers endure such a loss for the rest of their lives." He said all this without stopping for a breath of air.

"How large is that rug?" I asked, worn down yet genuinely interested, despite myself.

"I believe it is four feet by six feet, madam," he answered. The attendant reached for a tape measure.

"I'm six feet tall. Let's hold it up," I suggested. The two men lifted the carpet to my chin. "This rug is more like five feet long, but I'll take it, provided the price is right," I insisted.

"You can trust me, madam," he said, placing his hand over his heart. "With me, the price is always right, a gift price, really. You buy more carpets; I give you even better price. In fact, for you, I offer our best democratic price."

By the time negotiations were over, I was lighter on cash and owned two carpets, including his never-to-be-sold family heirloom.

His farewell rivaled his salesmanship: "Surely, your country must suffer your absence, madam. We will patiently await the day when you will visit us again."

Thankfully, Majid hurried me out of the shop. "We must go now to the Office of Tribal Authorities for our permits to trek within the restricted area."

Taking a circuitous route, our driver navigated the back streets and alleys of Peshawar to the Office of Tribal Authorities. While fumbling our way down a shadowy hallway to the Permits Department, Majid seemed increasingly uncomfortable. Once inside the office, we were met with measured hostility, as hefty men seated behind bulky desks scrutinized us. Majid had me take a seat on a plank bench against a wall, while he presented paperwork and answered an onslaught of questions, in Urdu. I didn't need to understand the words to see it wasn't going well—Majid shifted his weight from side to side as the officials grilled him. My presence didn't help. I stared through a dingy broken window, recalling the warm and gracious Minister of Expeditions in Islamabad. How easy it had been there. The inquiry ended abruptly with permits signed and approved. And, no, we did not pay them off.

Majid remained silent while he led us from the building. Only in the privacy of our jeep—our island of safety—did he grumble: unlike the Baltoro Glacier, here he was a total stranger. To make matters worse, the officials had thought he was a Westerner.

The road from Peshawar took us northward into the Northwest Frontier Province through an area of barren mountains and valleys bordering Afghanistan. Late in the day, we came to a lush river canyon and the town of Dir, deep in Sunni Fundamentalist country. "People here believe in strict adherence to the Koran and the total separation of sexes," Majid explained. When I asked how women felt about this, he replied, "Many *womens* share the same beliefs as their husbands. They choose to be completely covered. Fundamentalists reject Western ways as corrupting."

*The town of Dir*

No sooner had Majid answered, than a woman, draped in black fabric from head to toe, scurried along the roadside. I couldn't take my eyes off of her. I had read about such *burkas*, never expecting to actually see one. Her burka had only a tiny screened opening from which to look out. Two more women followed, one in a purple burka trimmed in fringe, and another in emerald green with tassels dangling at the forehead—these burkas had fashion. But then we passed one more woman, swaddled mummy-like in strips of white fabric, with only a narrow slit for her eyes. Unconsciously, my hand checked the positioning of my own veil. Strangely, I felt underdressed.

Passing two men with bright orange beards hanging below their chests, Majid again provided explanation: "What you are seeing are those people with the strictest beliefs. These men have made their pilgrimage to Mecca (the birthplace of the Prophet Muhammad). They show this by dying their beards orange."

We pulled up to a newly constructed guesthouse alongside the river and climbed its polished marble steps to a dark, empty lobby. "Do not worry. I will go and look for the manager," Majid said, leaving me there alone. I followed a shaft of daylight out onto a balcony overlooking the river, and waited. Below, a man stood waist deep in rushing water, digging up river mud, used to finish walls, much like plaster, Majid later told me.

The manager, a clean-shaven portly gentleman, arrived breathless and apologetic—he had been dealing with a power outage, he said. Then, because we were his only guests, he gave Majid a tour through each and every room.

"I have chosen a room for you I think you will like, Ruth," Majid said, returning from his tour. He ushered me to a suite directly off the lobby with its own private balcony. After approving the room, I wilted onto the bed and watched the ceiling lights flicker with each power surge.

At dinnertime, Majid returned for me. Once we were seated in the dining room, his voice shifted to a solemn tone. "I want to tell you what I have learned about the murder of your friend last year. I met with the police detective in charge of the case, and I was given access to the prison to speak with the criminals. They are very young— eighteen and twenty-three to be exact. Here is what they told me: They went up to your friend and said, 'You are not allowed here without a local guide. You are in a tribal area, which is restricted to foreign travel. You are camped too close to the tents of our wives and our children—you must move farther away from our families.' At first the two men offered to guide your friend, but he ordered them to leave. An argument broke out—they said he pulled a knife. They were frightened for their families. So they said, 'We will see you later!' They ran down to their village to get a gun. When they returned, they fired on the tent of your friend. I do not know if this was just a tragic misunderstanding due to language. Now, of course, they realize their mistake. They have been sentenced to twenty-five years in prison."

"Majid, why did you do this?" I asked, stunned by his actions and by the details of his account.

"Because I was so upset. This has happened in my country to someone you know. I had to find out why," he answered.

He switched to our upcoming trek. "We will hike along the border between Pakistan and Afghanistan, close to the ceasefire line established in the War with the Soviets. This area has been closed to foreigners for the past ten years. From there, we will continue along the Pamir Mountains of China and cross Chilinji Pass into a region of the Karakoram Mountains you have not seen. We will end in a valley of Hunza where foreigners have not been allowed to visit."

The next morning, as we thanked the guesthouse manager, he insisted I stand beside him while Majid snapped a quick photo of the two of us together. After saying good-bye a second time, the jeep whisked us away, rumbling along on a dirt road parallel to the river. Occasional breaks in the canyon afforded glimpses of irrigated valleys, framed by arid mountains. Our driver downshifted for the long pull to the top of Lawari Pass, altitude 10,230 feet, following the very route used by Alexander the Great when he invaded India in the fourth century BC—the same route used later by Genghis Khan, Cossacks, Huns, silk and slave traders. Here, the Silk Route bifurcated and continued northward along the Hindu Kush mountain range. *Hindu Kush* literally means *Hindu killer,* for the thousands of Hindu slaves who lost their lives attempting to cross.

When we reached the top of Lawari Pass, Majid had our driver stop. "May I present you the Chitral Valley," he said, pointing to the verdant Chitral River basin below, lined with amber poplars and encircled by mountains. "This road is closed seven months of the year due to snow. During those times, the only way to Chitral is through Afghanistan, the dry route. Between the Chitral District and Afghanistan, we have forty peaks over six thousand meters high (twenty thousand feet) with twenty-six passes; ancient caravan routes locals still use. In Chitral, we have six hundred thousand people. Half are refugees from Afghanistan. This is also the home of the Fundamentalist Islamic Police, who enforce the strictest practices of Islam."

"How?" I asked.

"They can come into a house and arrest a husband and wife for sitting at the same table," he replied, matter-of-factly. Before I could react, Majid jumped from the car, unaware his remark had left me reeling.

"Ruth, we can get out here, if you would like," he said. With some hesitation, I climbed from the jeep. This main artery looked abandoned—no roadside stands, no traffic, no animals—just dust. Much of the valley below was under cultivation and dotted with tawny huts, the color of the surrounding mountains.

*Typical dwellings in the Chitral valley*

"Ruth, I know how much you want to see Afghanistan. This is just like it. Here we have exactly the same people, and we can see typical Afghan homes, built in the traditional manner, using mud bricks. So we will go now, please." I paused, enjoying the views and the warm afternoon light. As the jeep began down the pass, Majid made a surprise announcement: "This morning the guesthouse manager told me about anti-American riots going on in Chitral."

*Great,* I thought.

"Yes, I am sorry we will not be able to see the city. We must go directly to our hotel. Our prime minister has been accused of treason for signing an agreement with your President Clinton, calling for the removal of the Mujahidin."

I remained silent.

"The manager told me these same protestors ransacked the office of the Aga Khan Foundation here two days ago," Majid added.

The Aga Khan seemed like an unlikely target. Said to be a descendant of the Prophet Muhammad and known for his long-held humanitarian commitment, his foundation underwrites the Aga Khan Rural Support Program, as well as education and healthcare centers in outlying areas. We'd passed several of his agricultural projects the year before—small plots of saplings, planted in some of the most remote and lifeless places imaginable—each with a sign crediting the Aga Khan Foundation.

"Protestors ransacked the Aga Khan's office? Why would he be a target?" I asked.

Majid shrugged and shook his head: "I do not know. These things just happen."

*A mosque along the Chitral River*

Our driver zipped through Chitral and directly to a wooden stockade gate. Tooting his horn, the gate opened to a walled courtyard. As soon as our jeep pulled inside, a gatekeeper slammed the gate shut and secured it with a bar. We swiftly left the jeep and immediately were whisked through a tiny lobby to an interior garden where white picket fences framed flower beds. After seeing to our check-in formalities, Majid joined me for tea. He seemed genuinely relieved to be there. "I think you will enjoy this hotel," he sighed. "It was once a British fortress."

Majid sipped his tea yet appeared distracted, agitated. After a long pause, he spoke. "This manager says there is a huge storm coming. The weather in the mountains to the north has been terrible— too much new snow and very cold."

We decided to delay our departure by a day. "We will use the time to visit the Kalash people who live in the Lost Canyons near here," Majid announced. "This is an isolated culture, whose roots we have not discovered. Some think they descended from Alexander the Great and his generals when they overtook the area. The Kalash dress in their own colorful manner, and *womens* do not cover their heads. They are the only non-Muslim culture in northern Pakistan. In fact, they hate Muslims and love Westerners. You will be very welcome there."

"Why do they hate Muslims?" I asked.

"Since 1976, when the road was built into their canyons, there have been cases of Muslim men going there and raping the *womens*. So they are very afraid. But now police guard the road to prevent this," he answered. "The drive will be easy—the road is good."

*A "good" road*

The "good road" amounted to a narrow swath, etched into a mountainside overhanging an enormous river gorge. "This will be the beginning of our interesting and exciting drive," Majid said, as we started toward the Lost Canyons. I watched our driver wrestle with the steering wheel, his elbows flying as he veered away from rocks and sections where the mountainside had slid away, leaving the roadbed hanging over open air. Meanwhile, Majid braced himself in his usual protective stance, stiff-armed with his hands pressed against the dashboard. By the time we arrived, I felt as though I'd been riding a galloping horse, nonstop, for days. It took nearly two hours to drive twenty miles.

A police checkpoint guarded the entrance to the canyons, said to be home to roughly three thousand Kalash people. After showing our papers, we proceeded into a seemingly idyllic setting of poplars, wildflowers, and cascading waterfalls, where children frolicked and women exchanged news over laundry.

A small fair-skinned girl darted between trees with a baby goat at her heels. When she saw us, she grabbed the animal in her arms and rushed to the roadside. Our driver slowed to a stop—the girl smiled, her green eyes sparkling. She wore a long black dress with a yoke embroidered in red and yellow, and multiple strands of colored beads around her neck. A red headpiece covered with cowry shells rested atop her braided hair; her earlobes were studded with turquoise nuggets. Tattooed to her cheeks were images of flowers—and between her eyebrows, a moon—a practice originally used to identify and reclaim women carried off by raiders, not unlike branded cattle.

*Kalash girl*

The goat, content in its owner's arms, hardly budged until our driver threw our jeep into gear. Then the animal's head popped up, exposing a turquoise earring hanging from one ear. Before we took off, a little boy ran to the girl's side with a myna bird riding on his shoulder. When it let out a squawk, Majid burst out laughing. "The bird has just greeted us in Urdu!"

Further into the canyon stood a cluster of whitewashed buildings, trimmed in wood and decorated with pictographs of encoded information we could only surmise. Animal, plant, and celestial images covered one hut, which was set apart from the others and surrounded by trees. "These people believe God exists in everything," Majid said, explaining the images. "*Womens* give birth in this hut. They stay here alone until the baby is born."

Nearby in another grove, weathered planks and dilapidated wooden boxes littered the ground. "These are the *caffeines,*" Majid said, quietly.

"*Caffeines?*" I repeated.

"Yes, this is where they place their dead—in open *caffeines* above ground. They leave them here, in the sun, where birds will come and eat them," he replied. The boxes contained whitened bones, and in one, cowry shells from the headdress of a woman laid to rest there.

*An open-air coffin holds bones and cowry shells of a Kalash woman laid to rest.*

The notion of birds metaphorically transporting the dead into afterlife exists in other areas of the Himalaya. In Tibet, Nepal, and Bhutan such open-air burials are known as sky burials. A body is hauled to a mountaintop and sometimes cut into pieces to enable birds (usually ravens) to carry the deceased away. If the birds fail to take the body, it is considered a bad omen, with a curse befalling not only the deceased, but all generations who follow.

# IV.

## NO TURNING BACK

### *Fear, the whisper between thoughts*

"It is good we had a day off because today will be a long drive to our trailhead—ten hours, perhaps twelve. This will be a very exciting jeep tour for you," Majid announced at breakfast.

*Not another* … my back ached at the mere mention of one more exciting jeep tour.

Sporting his turban and wraparound sunglasses, Majid crammed the last of our gear into the jeep. Soon, we were following the Chitral River canyon north, past tiny mountainside villages, which, from a distance, looked like brushstrokes of green on chamois walls. Majid acted as disc jockey, alternately playing traditional Pakistani music and American pop tunes on the jeep's tape deck. I pulled my veil tighter around my head to conceal my obvious Western appearance, a pointless gesture with Majid's favorite Bob Marley tape booming. Blaring our way through the canyon, we sounded like a political vehicle, in support of the wrong party. Throughout the day, we passed locals, who made hand gestures foreign to me, but unquestionably were hostile.

*Milky glacial water flows through a river basin along the Afghan border. Terraced fields and villages cling to the mountainside above.*

Late in the day, the road took us upward along a ledge above a vast river basin. What had been a fairly distinct jeep trail now deteriorated to a rut. A full can of gas sloshing behind me thumped against the back of my head. The drive began to feel like a roller coaster ride as our driver hit bumps and holes so fast, the jeep slid sideways into them. Each time, my head slammed into the ceiling, and the gas can whacked me from behind.

Not surprisingly, we had to stop to repair the jeep engine. Our driver took the gas can that had been banging against my head and poured fuel directly onto the engine while attempting to get it to fire, a technique I'd never seen. It worked—we were up and running again.

After hours of breathing gas fumes, dust, and exhaust, we stopped, having reached the end of the road, or more accurately, this round of physical assault. "We have come to our campsite," Majid said, as I rubbed my aching head. "Our trek will begin here."

Indeed, we had arrived at a vast alpine meadow with glaciers spilling down from surrounding peaks into a river basin below. Unloading our gear, we set up camp. Our driver would stay the night and not attempt the drive back until daybreak.

The next day, Majid's greeting sounded from just outside my tent: "Good morning, Ruth. Did you happen to bring duct tape with you? I have a hole in my tent."

"I'm sorry Majid, I didn't. What did you do with the roll I gave you last year?"

"I forgot it. Now please, would you happen to have a needle and thread?"

"Nope, not that either," I answered.

Majid wandered off, but not for long. "Do you have any rope? We need it for the cook tent." I produced a section of nylon cord.

"And would you happen to have a guide book?" he asked.

"That's it, Majid. I'm going home!" I teased.

I could hear Majid chuckle as he walked away. What I didn't realize at the time? He really did need a guide book.

I strolled out across the meadow. In the soft morning light, the grass glistened with frost, and the air hit me like a spring day. Goats foraged along the river's edge, wading through shallows to nibble on willows. In the distance stood the snow-covered Hindu Kush, dazzling in the morning sun.

*Herders and goats in a river basin along the Afghan border*

Back in camp, we had company—lots of company. Old men, swaddled in turbans, squatted together in a circle, idly drawing in the dust with their walking sticks. Gathered around our cook tent, a crowd of able-bodied men elbowed each other and craned their necks to catch a glimpse inside, where Majid conducted porter interviews. Lingering on the sidelines, young boys toting homemade slingshots and bows watched the action with great interest.

*Men crowd around the cook tent hoping to be hired as porters.*

A commotion broke out and exploded into an all-out brawl. Majid took control and ordered the instigator to leave. Slowly, camp settled down, and the group wandered off. Once we had the place to ourselves, I ventured over to the cook tent. "Majid, is there a problem with our being here?" I asked.

"Oh no, this was strictly an issue among locals," Majid explained. "That guy wanted to carry our loads the entire way, but these people have agreed to boundaries. Porters can only carry loads across one valley. Then, loads must be transferred to porters from the next valley. In this way, more people are able to work. He did not want to play by the rules."

"Who are these men?" I asked.

"Nomads from Afghanistan," Majid replied. "Pakistan has offered them a new life, allowing them to settle and graze their flocks in these valleys. They are also paid to patrol the border, since our government has no armed forces here. We call them War Zone Keepers. If they see anything unusual, they must run down the valley and report to the authorities. Some of these men are quite wealthy due to their herds."

"If they're wealthy, why would they want to work as porters?" I asked.

"For adventure," Majid answered. "This area has been closed for ten years due to the war with the Soviets—they have never seen a Westerner. What makes this trek so special is we can see this different culture. We have many surprising things here."

After breaking camp, we set out at a pleasant pace with our entourage of nine porters, six donkeys, and one yak. For a while, only the sound of breathing filled the crystalline air. Then Majid, cheerful as he loped along, broke out a flute and began playing folk tunes. A few hours passed before we noticed specks of red in the distance, fluttering about like confetti on an otherwise austere landscape. They turned out to be colorfully clad women, tending their goats. I asked Majid if we could visit.

*Afghan refugee women tend their goats near the Afghan border.*

"Why not? I will ask one of our porters to speak with them." Majid dispatched a runner, who returned with permission.

We strolled over to their cluster of mud-and-sod huts. Nearby, yak dung had been laid out to dry—a precious fuel for burning in this treeless landscape. Hay had been piled high on rooftops, away from hungry livestock. A yak tethered to a stake, stared with blank eyes while others, sensing its disadvantage, ventured only close enough to goad it.

As soon as we came near, the women pulled their veils around their faces and rushed to the far corner of a rock-enclosed animal pen. Only one elderly woman remained, holding a toddler. Proud to show off her granddaughter, she smiled, while the others—some teenagers, nursing infants—began to relax. Returning to their chores, they occasionally paused to study us. A few even dropped their veils and timidly smiled. Majid spoke with the older woman and translated: "This is all one family. They fled Afghanistan to escape Taliban cruelty. Now, they come to this valley from Chitral every summer with their flocks. The men see to the cattle, while the *womens* stay with the children and goats."

*Having adjusted to strangers, Afghan girls lower their veils.*

*Afghan refugee family near the border of Afghanistan*

Before we parted ways, they were posing for family photos. In the end, I think they honestly enjoyed the visit. We left them to their privacy and continued on. Soon we found ourselves in an expansive field of marijuana, interspersed among rows of sweet peas. Majid picked a handful of peas to sample. Cracking pods, we ate our way to a small barnyard, jammed with livestock. The farmer, Babu, gave us permission to camp there. His animals, curious and hungry, sniffed our bags as we unpacked and followed me everywhere. We spent the night with those animals. Never sleep downwind from a yak.

Early in the morning, the sound of men arguing and shouting woke me up. Majid explained how a new group of porters had stormed into camp, insisting on carrying our loads. The entire valley was free for anyone to graze their herds, but when it came to doing carries, this crew wouldn't let anyone else work their area. Majid reacquainted all parties with the terms: in accordance with the local agreement, our first porters, having reached the end of their ferry zone, would be sent home, each with a one-hundred-rupee tip, the amount specified by Majid. Only the yak would stay behind. A trader, coming soon over the pass from Gilgit, planned to buy three hundred goats from Babu and needed a yak as well. Babu agreed to try to sell the animal for the departing owner.

Unlike the Baltoro Glacier trek, where the same Balti porters accompanied us from beginning to end, this arrangement gave us more opportunities to meet locals. These porters were Sunnis—they were kind, loyal, respectful, always smiling, and above all, phenomenally strong.

Midmorning, when we were about to leave, Babu disappeared into his hut. When he came back out, he had swapped his turban and salwar kameez for western wear—cowboy style. Decked out in blue jeans, rawhide belt, collared shirt, leather vest, and hat, he swaggered toward us, while casually donning aviator sunglasses to top off his look. He'd be leaving his harvesting, he announced, to personally accompany us across his valley. Mounting an impressive horse, he struck a pose and swung around in the direction of the route.

Off we went, walking for six hours without seeing a single other person besides our own group. We were within a mile of the Afghan border, travelling through an area called The Door, a passage between Afghanistan and Pakistan occupied by the Soviets during their war with Afghanistan.

*Passing through The Door, a region along the Afghan border occupied by the Soviets during their war with Afghanistan.*

"You are from America. You are from the strongest country in the world. When will America come and help us?" a voice called out from the russet folds of landscape.

Majid froze, his eyes locked forward in the direction of the voice. "Word must have traveled ahead," he murmured.

We never learned who shouted, yet my senses told me they always knew where we were. There had been no Westerners through this area since the War with the Soviets, Babu said.

When we happened upon a Soviet hospital bed parked alongside a solitary mud hut, Majid translated as Babu told us about the area. "So this place is very interesting in the historical text. Here, the Soviets had full power, which is to say they had modern weapons and were frightening all these poor people settled up here. This was quite serious because the Soviets were testing big guns, like rocket launchers. They sent their young recruits—the new soldiers just getting into the military—for exercising here and stranded them. Many soldiers starved and died. Today, we can still see farmers using things the Soviets left behind, like broken rifles, eating bowls, and crashed helicopter parts."

For several days, we crossed idyllic high-altitude pastures and rivers that ran through them, fed from all sides by the glaciated peaks of the Hindu Kush. During those days, we never saw another settlement, but we did pass the ruins of a fortress, abandoned after Britain's failed attempt to colonize Afghanistan in the mid-1800s. *No one—not even Alexander the Great—has ever succeeded in conquering Afghanistan,* I thought.

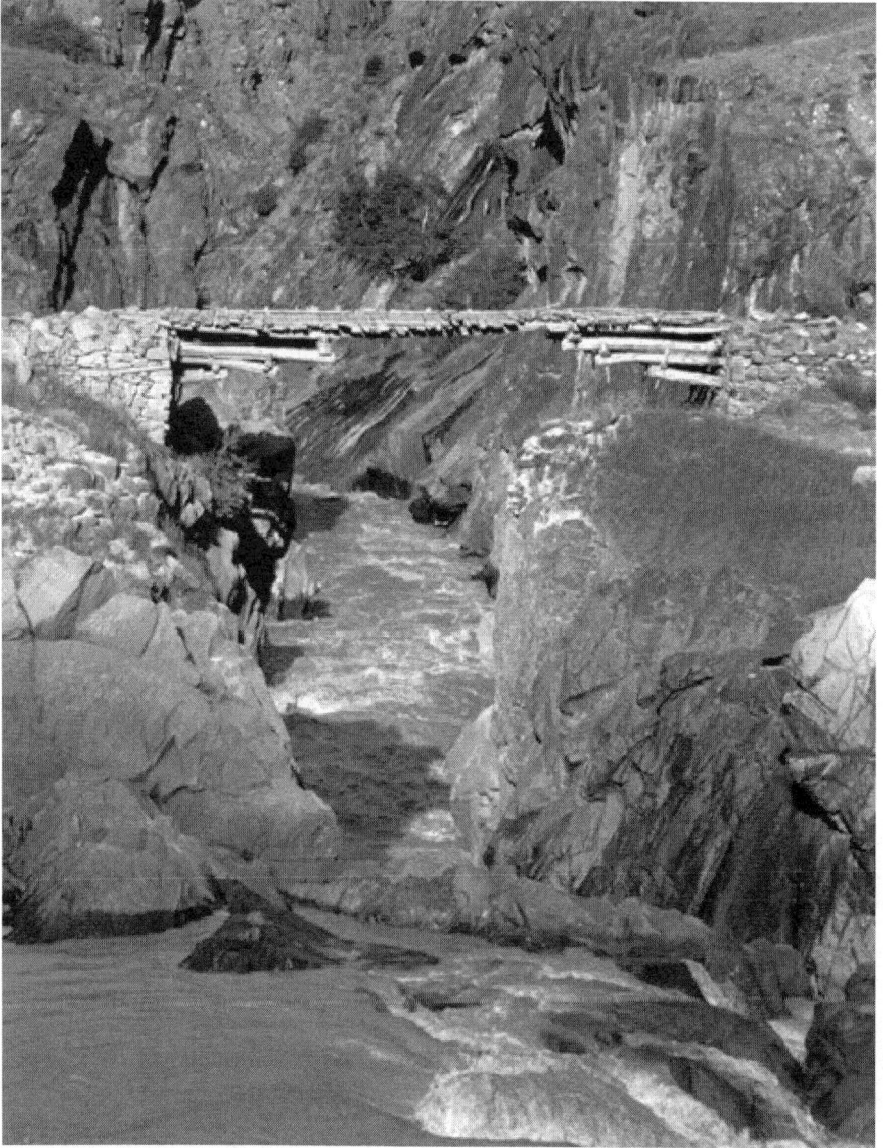

*A bridge, held together by wooden pins, is anchored by rock ramps.*

On our eighth day, after walking four hours through open meadowlands, we came to an aqua-blue lake fed by a huge jewel-like wall of ice, a sacred lake, according to Babu. Again, Majid translated: "We have come to a most exciting point called, *Ischawars,* which means Holy Sand. This is where a flying horse once jumped onto the Holy Sand

and formed this lake. You can still see the horse footprints on the water."
He pointed to a recurring string of ringlets on the water's surface,
resulting from a series of underwater springs bubbling up sequentially. I
wondered if this flying horse might be the wind horse depicted on prayer
flags in Tibet, Nepal, Ladakh, and Bhutan. I had once been told that the
wind horse represents the human soul in the shamanism of Central Asia.

I held back for a moment at the lake's edge and listened to the
water lap at my feet. Lacy ice crystals clung to blades of tundra grass,
and a spectacularly glaciated peak rose from the opposite shore.
Overhead, a lone eagle circled effortlessly without seeming to move a
muscle. From somewhere on the ground, a marmot, wary of its
predator, whistled an alarm.

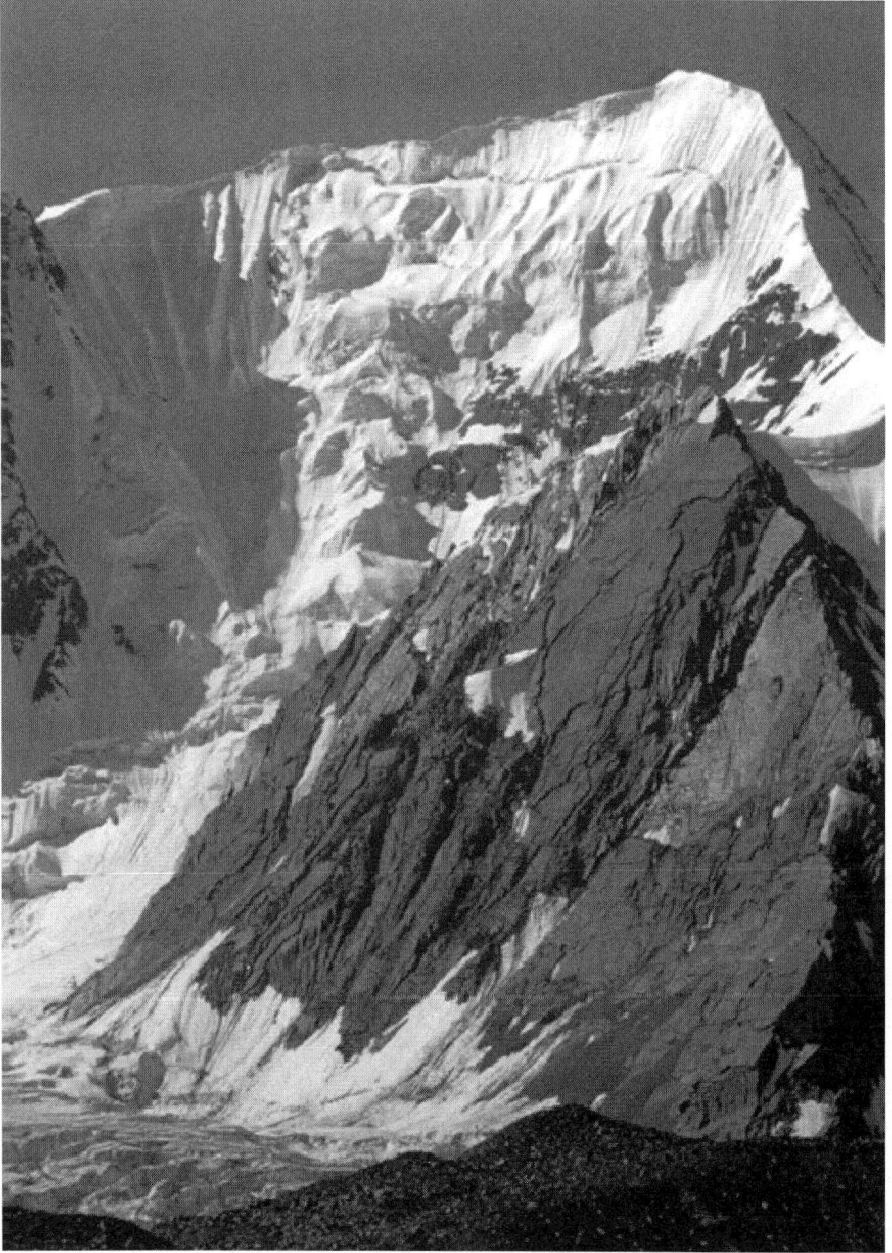

*Glaciated Pamir peak*

By late afternoon we stopped to camp, having reached an elevation of 12,600 feet. Even before we'd finished unloading, locals were coming to visit—they just appeared, seemingly out of nowhere. For days, we had not seen another soul, not passed a single dwelling or so much as a tree, only wide open, high-altitude grassland—tundra, really. Either we were trekking slowly, or word had travelled ahead fast. I had the feeling these people had been close by all the way without our knowing.

"Here, we are near the region of the Pamir Mountains and Afghanistan, known as the Wakhan Corridor," Majid explained. "*Wakhan* means *wall between two states*. These locals, called Wakhis, are the same people who settled upper Hunza, but their roots are in Afghanistan. They are now refugees from Afghanistan, but before they were nomads who wandered back and forth between Afghanistan and Pakistan. For thousands of years, these mountains have kept this area isolated and divided into rival valleys—natural fortresses—with local warlords locked in power struggles. Only when faced with a common enemy, like the Soviets, do tribes bond together as allies. Afterwards, it is back to tribal squabbles, as usual. For the past seven years these tribal guys have been allowed to own property in Pakistan. Now, if these guys spot trouble, they must run to an army post and inform the authorities."

"So tomorrow, we will leave the Northwest Frontier Territory and enter the Pamir Mountains through an area that was once part of China but now is independent," Majid continued. "And tonight, Babu leaves us to return home." This was a concern: Babu seemed to be the only person out here who knew the way.

Late in the afternoon, Babu asked Majid if I could take a photo of him mounted on his horse. Everyone crowded around the horse, anxious to have their picture taken, too. Not to be outdone, Majid, adjusting his Karakoram cowboy hat, asked Babu to let him pose on the horse. Swinging into the saddle, the horse caught him by surprise, taking off in a full gallop and barreling straight toward me with wide-eyed Majid gripping both the mane and halter. When the animal came to a stop, Majid couldn't wait to dismount. In turn, each porter mounted up, hoping to set his own land speed record.

As much out of concern for the horse as our porters, I rounded everyone up for a group photo. They fell into formation—all except the last rider who was unwilling to relinquish his turn. He reined in the horse and stood upright on the saddle, like a circus performer. I barely had time to click one frame before he lost his balance and crashed to the ground. In the end, all cowboys limped off, complaining of groin injuries. *Too much horsing around, I guess.*

Knowing his horse was his pride and joy, I presented Babu with a roll of bright yellow webbing—a flat, woven-nylon strapping used in mountaineering. I thought there might be enough to make a flashy halter and rein for his horse. Majid translated while I ran the idea by Babu, who seemed thrilled. Before we bid farewell to Babu, a new group of men had already congregated—our soon-to-be porters, this time with high-altitude yaks.

By morning, a black cloud had crept down a side canyon and settled on the ground, obscuring visibility. Our route led directly into it. For the better part of the day, we wandered through murky fog, eventually traversing a wall where water surged from a slit "as though here, the rock had been slashed by a dagger," to use Majid's description. Crossing the waterway would require pulling ourselves hand-over-hand while riding in a metal basket suspended from a pulley and cable. But there was a problem—part of the pulley system was missing. "Locals sometimes carry parts away to keep people from entering their territory," Majid said.

After sizing up the situation, Majid announced, "I have decided to camp here. Tomorrow morning, when the water is lower, we will ride yaks across."

Later in the evening, our porters held a goat festival. Recalling how our Balti porters had done this to ensure their safety before climbing onto the Baltoro Glacier, I wondered aloud what to expect. This is when Majid told me he had never been here before.

*Razor-edged ridgelines in the Hindu Kush mountains*

The next morning, I awoke to the sound of yaks grunting just outside my tent and another beautiful, crystal clear, blue-sky morning. As our porters loaded their yaks for the river crossing, I asked Majid how much weight each animal could carry.

"Six-hundred kilograms," Majid replied.

"That's over a thousand pounds." I said.

"Yes, they are very strong. So please, Ruth, the porter will help you onto a yak now." I wondered if this was going to be like riding Titan, the mechanical bull at Gilley's.

I strapped on my pack. A porter tried to boost me onto a yak, but it spooked and bolted away. We tried again. This time, I managed to grab on and claw my way through yak hair until I balanced uncomfortably, directly over the animal's protruding spine. Gripping his wide body with my legs, I had nothing else to cling to except fur, and no long neck to catch me in a forward fall—a yak's neck is short and usually angled downward.

The yak swayed back and forth across loose rock, stumbling often. The shallow decline of the riverbank felt like a cliff—I fully expected either to end up skewered on his long horns or to hit the ground headfirst, with a view looking straight up a yak nostril. The river didn't seem threatening until the water reached chest-high on the animal, when even this beast had trouble fighting the current. While I tried to anticipate which way to dive if we went down together, Titan and I safely reached the other side.

*A porter and wet yak after a river crossing*

As we trekked northward and climbed higher, the riverbank turned to ice. Rounding a blind corner, we came upon a blockade of fractured ice spanning an entire valley, one mile across. The sight took my breath away.

"Today we will cross a small glacier," Majid said, almost to himself, "… a very small glacier."

*Small glacier? Who's he kidding? Nothing about this place is either small or tame.* I didn't know what trip Majid thought he was on, but I was beginning to realize what trip I was on—the wrong trip. No need to ask about Plan B …

"It will take only one hour to cross. Do not worry," he added.

Who was worried? Never mind that we had no proper gear—no crampons, ropes, or ice axes to safely attempt such a glacier crossing. Wearing their rubber shoes with zero tread—their soles were perfectly smooth—our porters climbed right up onto the ice. But our yaks froze in terror until our porters beat them into obedience, a tough ordeal to watch.

*Negotiating crevasses on the "small" glacier*

When it came my turn, the slick ice instantly threw me. I flailed and contorted in configurations and recoveries, more marionette-like than human. Luck kept me upright, as did pebbles and grit, which provided a little traction. But as the sun warmed the icy surface, those same rocks loosened up and acted like ball bearings. Losing my balance one more time, I bit my lip. Any mistake here could be my last.

*Porters and animals skirt crevasse drop-offs while crossing the "small" glacier.*

*Never assume things are so bad they can't get worse.* The very emotion needed to keep any rational person from attempting this insane crossing was the very emotion needed to succeed—fear. Never had I felt so vulnerable, so exposed; each step was an act of faith. Straddling a line between nothing and nothing, I crept along spines of ice that dropped in eighty-degree plunges off either side into black holes from which there could be no recovery, because we had no rescue equipment. *Don't give in to fear or you're gone. Focus, commit, and move forward—hesitation kills.*

*Of the climbers who disappear into crevasses, half are never recovered,* whispered the voice. A moot point, given our only rope was a hemp yak lead, looped around one porter's neck in such a way that it surely would have strangled him had he fallen in.

*Crevasses separated by spines of ice*

At one point, I saw Ismail straining to extend his hand to me as he balanced on a nipple of ice in his pitiful rubber shoes. I didn't know if he needed help or was trying to help me—I couldn't get close enough. I tried, but never reached him. So easily we could have gone down together in this hand-to-hand culture.

Three hours after starting across the ice, we made it to a rock mound on the opposite side. We had begun the crossing with three yaks, one donkey, and nine porters. Miraculously, we still had everyone. I was beyond words after being caught so totally off guard. I'd been on many glaciers, but this was by far the most frightening. My knees were weak. After so much adrenaline, all I felt was relief. *Next time, I'll imagine the unthinkable ... and maybe come up prepared.*

The following morning, a commotion outside my tent woke me up. Propping myself on one elbow, I peeked through the tent flap. Outside towered a gang of bearded, dark-skinned giants. I counted eight men in all. Most were well over six feet tall; three were almost seven feet. With yak-hair ropes crisscrossing their chests, they looked like freedom fighters. These were Pashtuns, the dominant tribe of Afghanistan. They had outlined their eyes in black, a practice common among graduates of the fundamentalist Madrassas who ended up as Taliban fighters. The one exception was a short, ruddy-faced man who had a red beard and piercing green eyes. With a wool turtleneck worn over his salwar kameez, he could almost have passed for a Scottish gentleman out for a jaunt. At his side stood five of the tiniest donkeys I'd ever seen.

*So these must be our new porters,* I thought, zipping the tent shut.

I didn't care who they were. These guys knew the way out of here. Majid didn't—he'd never been here before. I decided I'd follow food, fuel, and local knowledge. If our porters turned back, I'd turn back. But secretly, I wondered how much these men would risk for a Western woman.

*A porter spins a yak-hair rope using a drop spindle.*

When I arrived to the cook tent for breakfast, Majid and Ismail were in deep discussion about arranged marriage. I sat down quietly as Majid lamented its shortcomings. "The day after my wedding, I was playing with a firecracker that blew up in my hand. My wife got so mad. She told me, 'You act like a child.' I told her, 'Hundreds of people tell me this!' She just got madder. Sometimes arranged marriages save problems, sometimes not."

Pulling out his wallet, Majid produced a photo of a pretty, fair-skinned girl with green eyes and sandy-brown hair. She stood, unveiled, in a garden. "This is my wife. I saw her only once before we married, when I was a young child. I saw her again on my wedding day. My parents picked out a woman and, being agreeable, I said yes. Here, marriage is not always about romance. It is an economic contract that binds families and determines inheritance."

"Are all marriages arranged?" I asked.

He looked to Ismail and laughed. "Ismail says he had a marriage by love!" For some reason Majid and the porters found this uproariously funny.

"Is it a problem to be married to someone outside the Muslim culture?" I asked.

"No, Ruth, here it is quite common for Muslim men, but not for Muslim *womens*. Because Islam is transferred from father to child, children of Muslim men are considered Muslim from birth. Muslim *womens* who marry outside the faith break this line."

While we were talking, a shepherd and his young son stopped by. The shepherd offered Majid a gift—ten lumps of a yellow substance, wrapped in burlap—goat cheese, I later learned. The boy had white-blond hair. When I commented on his looks, Majid explained, "Here in the Pamir, we are very close to the former Soviet Union. After the crack-up of the U.S.S.R., there are now four independent states: Uzbekistan, Tajikistan, Kazakhstan, and Kyrgyzstan. Many of those people have migrated from all over the Pamir Plateau into Pakistan. They look different from other locals and have their own unique cultures. Even their way of greeting is different from ours."

After breakfast, we loaded up and began moving upstream. Shortly, we came to a rock dwelling where a small boy stood in the doorway. When he saw us, he rushed inside. Two men emerged, an older gentleman in a threadbare coat, and a younger man. They looked Mongolian. The boy trailed behind them, toting his baby sister.

*Boy from Tajikistan and his sister*

When Majid greeted them, the elder broke into a toothless grin beneath his long white mustache. We learned they were from Tajikistan. During the Soviet era, Tajikistan's food and fuel had been subsidized by the U.S.S.R. After the fall of the Soviet Block, subsidies stopped, forcing people to leave rather than face starvation. Their new life here seemed consumed only with the business of survival.

Saying good-bye, we pressed on. Along the way, we occasionally encountered other family clusters—one clan had bright red hair and green eyes. This corridor seemed to be a melting pot of people left behind during previous migrations.

*Laundry dries on the ground outside a dwelling along the Afghan border. Animal fodder is stored on rooftop.*

We heard the rapids long before we came to the next river. As we drew closer, the air actually felt charged with electricity. Then we saw them: four raging tributaries of one raging river. "Here we can see where the river made a huge damn and exploded like a water bomb," Majid said. A landslide had wiped out the bridge we were supposed to cross.

*A sapling bridge, held together by wooden pins, is suspended from rock ramps.*

"We must make an unscheduled river crossing," Majid announced.

Our porters began removing their shoes. I started to do likewise, but Majid stopped me. "No, Ruth, it will not be necessary to take off your boots. One of our porters has offered to carry you across." Majid pointed to Sami, our red-bearded, green-eyed porter, who smiled and nodded.

"But I'm too heavy for him," I objected.

"You will see," Majid replied, grinning.

Clearly, there would be no talking them out of this. With his pants rolled up, exposing legs that looked like a muscle overlay from an anatomy book, Sami summoned me onto his back. I grabbed the rope slung over his shoulders and jumped on board, expecting at least to hear a groan. Instead, he strode out into the water. As the river deepened, I could feel its force pounding against this man, smaller than I, up to his waist in rushing water, with me on his back. It was unbelievable. Step by step, Sami cut through the icy current until we had crossed all four branches. What's more, he did it barefooted.

That evening, I kicked off my boots and crawled into a corner of our cook tent while I waited for dinner. When Majid joined me, I was trying to find a comfortable position for my long legs that wouldn't expose the bottoms of my feet to view, an act considered insulting to Muslims. With the lantern set on the ground, the light threw unnatural shadows upward, onto Majid's face. Ismail entered just behind him—he looked weird, too. I squinted at both men—they looked like they were wearing eyeliner.

"OK, you guys. What have you done to your eyes?" I asked.

Majid seemed a bit sheepish as he explained, "Our porters have showed us how the guys up here grind a black stone. Then, they put the powder into a small tool and draw around their eyes."

At first I said nothing. Only the most extreme *Mujahidin* did this, so I'd heard. The look was startling: their eyes appeared adrenaline-filled, larger than normal, and with whites that seemed to jump right out. "You guys look wild," I said.

They threw reassuring glances to each other. I left them to the company of Majid's tape player and Kenny G. The yaks, lying just outside, grunted in perfect rhythm.

Predictably, by morning Majid had an eye infection. One eye had swollen entirely shut, with the other on its way.

"My eye is like a rock! I was awake half the night," he whined, rubbing his eye.

"Majid, leave it alone, and don't rub it," I said, examining his puffy eye.

To my utter astonishment, Majid exploded into a tirade of anger. Then, to my complete bewilderment, he blamed his problem on the women goat herders we'd passed a week ago: "Those damn *womens*! At their village I looked upon the rags of menses. They were on the ground in a pile, where I could not avoid seeing them. It is a sin to look upon this blood, and Allah punishes it severely. Now, this curse has come upon me!"

No way would I be tackling this subject. After he'd finished raging and calmed down, I simply suggested he not use any more off the black stuff. Just a thought ...

Five hours into our day's hike, we crested a hill, where goats peeked out from brush to study us, their heads cocked to one side. I stopped for a moment to enjoy their antics and to take in the stunning view of the Pamir mountain range. We ambled down the path to an intensifying sound of roaring water. Coming nearer, I could feel the force vibrate through the ground. The river turned out to be fifty yards wide.

A rickety metal basket dangled from a rusty wheel that skipped along a frayed cable, spanning the river, "a recent advancement," according to Majid. "Cables used to be made from willow twigs braided together."

Sami had already arrived and tied his rope to the basket. Jumping into the contraption, he began crossing the span by pulling himself along the cable hand-over-hand. I eyed the way the metal wheel wobbled across. The cable sagged and rebounded, allowing the rushing water to smack the basket each time it dropped.

After Sami had reached the opposite bank, two anchormen on our side pulled the empty rig back, using the rope. They signaled me to climb in. Sami hauled me across, a process repeated until all but three porters were left on the far bank. They had stayed behind with our donkeys. Tying rope around each animal's neck, they shoved the animals into the water. Instantly, the current swept them downriver. For a moment, I could see the whites of their eyes, then only muzzles. Once the rope stretched tight, they completely disappeared underwater. Our porters fought to keep their footing as they dragged the animals crosscurrent to shore. First, one hoof surfaced, then another. Struggling, our waterlogged donkeys clambered onto the rock bank, shivering and snorting.

With my focus on the animals, I hadn't noticed a group of villagers gathered behind us. An angry white-bearded elder presided over them. His identical twin stood at his side, his face mirroring the same internal rage. They were clearly not there to welcome us. At first they spoke in stern tones. With no warning, the situation escalated into a shouting match, directed at Sami. The elders were fighting mad, and they were ferocious. I backed away, not understanding the issue, and hoping I hadn't caused it. I thought perhaps we had violated some territorial boundary unknown to us, or worse, my presence had offended and incensed them.

Majid tried to intervene, but got caught in the crossfire. The clash continued for fifteen minutes until Majid persuaded the villagers to sit down and hold a *jirga,* a meeting to make sense of what had just happened. Thirty minutes of intense discussion passed before they finished.

*A elder listens during the jirga.*

"The argument was about the rope used to cross the river," Majid told me afterward. "Our government has hired Sami to erect and maintain this cable system. The rope he carries is to pull the box across the river—he is supposed to keep the rope with him so no one will steal it. These people did not understand. They were angry because they thought the rope should be in place at all times. They have been stranded on this side of the river and had to tie together bits of old rope to get back across. The elders say it is too dangerous for their families. They thought Sami did this to them on purpose. But we have explained the truth to them. Sometimes it is impossible to know about these local issues," he added, shrugging.

*An elder oversees village men as they rig their pulley basket to cross the river.*

Before I had time to process all that had transpired, the elder led us to what looked like a stack of tree cuttings, covered with a canvas tarp. Ducking inside through a small opening, he returned with a carpet he unrolled, inviting the men to sit down. Then, he gestured for me to enter the inner sanctum of the tarp-covered structure.

I wasn't about to say no.

*Juniper branches and a canvas tarp form the walls and roof of a lodge-pole dwelling.*

In the stifling smoke-filled darkness, details began to take shape, illuminated only by embers glowing in a small fire pit. The structure consisted of lodge-pole timbers, lashed together at the top and anchored with boulders on the ground. Over this frame, junipers had been stacked to form the walls and roof, with a tarp draped across the top for extra protection. Water bottles and slabs of meat hung from juniper boughs, also clothing and rifles. Soot-covered pots lined the fire pit, and near the pit, a bloated goat carcass stood stiff and lifeless on all fours. Totally out of place in this surrounding was a floral-pattern china bowl set off to one side.

Throwing her veil over her shoulder to keep it from the fire, an older woman directed me to sit next to her. She seemed excited to have company, and only because the elder had permitted it. She poured water from the goat carcass into a teapot. While baking chapatti, she kept one eye on a large pot of boiling goat milk. To her side, a young mother in her teens nursed an infant. When she turned my way, the firelight illuminated a radiant face, framed in a red veil. Across from us sat a little girl and teenaged boy, who simply stared at me.

The woman served me first, warm chapatti slathered with goat butter. With all eyes watching, I had no choice but to take a bite. I smiled and nodded appreciatively. She filled the china bowl with tea, added a ladle of goat milk, and shoved it under my nose. I stared at the bowl and smiled again. Doomed, I feigned a sip. But one sip wasn't enough—she wanted me to finish it. The minute I emptied the bowl, she refilled it.

Once again, all eyes were on me. I felt like the afternoon television show. I forced another smile, stared at the pink roses painted around the rim, and took fleeting comfort in those details so foreign to this place. Again, the woman insisted. Again, I downed the tea. Again, she refilled the bowl and pushed it into my face.

My eyes burned—I needed to cough. I gulped tea, chewed on chapatti, and counted the ways I could die a normal death. I had to escape, and do it gracefully. In my awkward Urdu, I thanked my hostess for her hospitality, stood up, and left.

The minute I stepped back into daylight, I popped an antibiotic. Naturally, I tried to do this without anyone noticing. But one man on the carpet spotted me, and a buzz instantly swept through the group and back to Majid. "Ruth, they want to know if you have medicine for aching hands." I pulled out aspirin and dispensed tablets. Another villager tugged on Majid's sleeve with his request: "This man needs medicine for his wife who is sick with fever, headaches, and a deep cough in her chest." More aspirin. All of a sudden, everyone with sniffles or aches lined up for pills. But when they brought me a sick donkey, it was time to move on. Walking and healing ...

*The Pashtun elder poses with his male children.*

Before we managed to pull away from the crowd, Majid bought a goat for our porters—our second goat this trip. There seemed to be a pattern developing: whenever we were about to do something dangerous, our porters sacrificed a goat. The Baltoro Glacier had only been a one-goat trip. But now I realized the Baltoro had only been the warm up. This was already a two-goat trip

By the time we left the village, dark clouds had enveloped the peaks, the wind had intensified, and snow had begun to fall. "We have spent too much time here. I am anxious to reach camp before this storm blows in," Majid said, picking up the pace.

Majid and our porters charged off with the donkeys while I hung back with Ismail, who didn't feel well and also wasn't sure of the way. He seemed worried as we bushwhacked up a heavily forested gulch and zigzagged back and forth, searching for any hint of a trail, and not sure which direction to go. We had to keep moving to stay ahead of the front. At last, we heard noise in the distance. Following the sound, we found our way to camp.

"That is Chilinji Pass!" Majid announced when we arrived, pointing to an opening in the clouds above.

"All I see is a wall," I responded.

"That is it," he repeated, again pointing upward to a rock face, over eighteen thousand feet in elevation. "Tomorrow, it will only take one hour to cross … or maybe three," he said, clearing his throat.

That evening, Majid soaked his eyes with a rag boiled in water, while our porters began dressing out the goat. They heaped dry brush in a huge pile and poured lantern fuel directly onto the open flames from a can held only inches above the growing fire. In a burst their fire exploded into a bonfire, with flames leaping well into the tree limbs overhead. I wondered how to say, "Run! Fire!" in Urdu.

Instinctively I moved away, as did our donkeys. I watched the pyrotechnics from a safe distance, while our animals milled about, their silhouettes backlit by firelight. The bonfire crackled and sparked, sending embers dancing and drifting skyward. Some spiraled; others shot out into darkness like heat-seeking missiles, lighting up the night sky for an instant. Above us, the stars seem closer than normal. Somehow, I felt a part of everything out there.

"Those porters sat around the fire all night long, singing and playing drums," complained Majid when he came to wake me in the morning, as though I might somehow have slept through the festivities. "Today we move to high camp. Their goat festival will bring them good luck on the pass."

I now had diarrhea, for good luck. Germs seemed to be the only living things thriving in this environment. As I wondered how many words Urdu has for *diarrhea*, I unzipped the tent door to greet my leader. Majid's eyes were practically swollen shut.

"Yes, I am having trouble seeing over my lower eyelid," he whined.

"I have eye drops—they may help. I'll bring the bottle to breakfast," I offered.

While treating Majid's eyes, he winced and pulled away. I thought perhaps I had hurt him.

"No, my tooth hurts," he groaned, rubbing his jaw.

"Your tooth?"

"Yes, last night while I fought with a bone (goat), I bit down so hard, I lost my temporary filling. Now the tooth is very painful."

"How long have you had the temporary filling?" I asked.

"My dentist put it in six months ago and told me to come back and see him right away," he answered.

"And?"

"I did not do it."

"OK, my dentist gave me some special stuff I carry on treks for this very reason. It's like putty—it will fill the hole and keep it from hurting until you can see your own dentist," I said.

Grabbing my first-aid kit, I met Majid in the cook tent. "Here, this will fix you for now." I squeezed a small glob from a tube onto his finger, and watched as he nervously found the hot spot. "Now, push it down into the hole, Majid."

After his pain had subsided and he felt like talking, Majid shared details of an emergency dental procedure he'd once performed: "One time on the Baltoro Glacier, we had a porter with such a terrible toothache! I had to use the corkscrew on my Swiss Army knife to dig out this guy's tooth. Then, I filled the hole with chewing tobacco to stop the bleeding." Majid seemed quite proud of his feat.

And with this, my breakfast ended.

Outside, our porters had already loaded the donkeys and were restless to leave. These were the smallest donkeys—with fragile little legs—and still they carried incredible loads.

"The route to the glacier will be gentle," Majid said.

The route turned out to be anything but gentle. We struck out on a course that took us upward into an amphitheater-like basin with steep walls. As soon as we were out of the trees, the wind picked up, and rain turned to hail, pelting and stinging exposed skin. From there, the slope increased to a seventy-degree incline of mud, gravel, and rock—more a climb than a hike. Feeling weak, I put my head down and pushed onward.

Suddenly, one of our donkeys keeled over onto her side. Two porters rushed to the animal's aid, removing her load and lifting her upright. Raw flesh hung from her trembling haunches; blood covered her legs. While our porters redistributed the donkey's load to their own backs, Sami stroked and tried to calm her. He spoke softly; Majid translated. "The wound is quite serious. Sami is worried the animal may die. These are his brother's donkeys—he feels personally responsible for them."

"Should we turn around?" I asked.

"No. From this point on, there can be no turning back," Majid replied.

"When we get to camp, I have medicine and bandages. They may help," I offered.

"Thank you, I will tell Sami. But now we must keep going—we are getting soaked."

Slogging up narrow icy paths of loose rock and through snow and boulder fields, we crossed onto the glacier where we would spend the night. Our high camp sat directly below Chilinji Pass, which separates the Pamir and Karakoram mountain ranges. Cold and exhausted, we staggered into camp.

Ismail, coughing and wheezing, prepared tea for everyone. I asked how he felt. He nodded and smiled—his face, drawn and pale. Despite the cold air, I noticed beads of perspiration on his forehead. "Ismail, you must rest tonight. Here, I want you to take these pills now." I pulled out my bottle of aspirin and shook two into his hand. He nodded appreciatively.

When I spotted Sami examining his injured donkey, I grabbed my med kit and stood by his side, ready to assist. The animal had a large gash on her rump and another on a front leg. I pulled out a bottle of antiseptic, soaked each wound, and wrapped the animal's leg with gauze, while Sami watched intently over my shoulder. After I had done what little I could, I gave him the remaining medicine and bandages so he could carry on after we parted ways.

Later, Majid showed up at my tent door. "Ruth, here is your dinner. It is too windy to put up the cook tent."

"Thank you, Majid. How is Ismail?" I asked, reaching out for the tray.

"He is resting now. He will be fine. Do not worry," Majid answered.

"I am worried about him. His cough sounds awful," I said.

"He is very strong, Ruth. I will watch him tonight," he responded. "Tomorrow, we will start up the pass early. The snow will only be knee deep. Do not worry."

*Every time he says not to worry, I worry. Sure hope the weather lets up. At this point, there's no turning back—we'll be crossing the pass regardless.*

I played with my food, having lost my appetite to altitude. Throughout the night, while wrestling with my own stomach cramps, I listened to Ismail's deep raspy cough, which I could hear from all the way across camp.

*So here we are, in a remote place within a remote country, surrounded by ragged peaks shooting upward, like teeth on a massive saw. Here, where walking is the only form of transportation, we have two choices: wait out winter, or press on.*

Morning wake-up came at four o'clock with tea and bread. We bundled up, pulled on our boots, and set out across a field of new snow two-feet deep, which, despite the darkness, seemed to emit a soft blue light. The sky had cleared, causing temperatures to plummet—the Milky Way looked like bits of glass in a kaleidoscope, catching and reflecting pinpoints of light. As we started up the first of many switchbacks, the bitter-cold air singed my lungs.

An hour slipped by. To the west, the shadow of the earth—cast against its own atmosphere—colored the predawn sky in a wash of magenta, shifting to lavender the closer it dropped to the horizon.

At last, the sun.

The footpath was so steep, I could look straight down onto the tops of our porters' heads as they passed below me on the switchbacks. Using sapling walking sticks, they climbed steadily, despite the weight of their massive loads. None of them had adequate clothing: they wore shoes stuffed with plastic bags to keep their feet dry, and not one man had gloves. Instead, they pulled their sleeves down over their hands.

Another hour slipped by. Mountaineers joke about leaving their brains in base camp—*wish I hadn't left mine.* My stomach felt like a bubble in a lava lamp. We had a thousand feet to go, and the going was getting tougher. Majid had said it would be an easy climb, a good trail. It was neither. Walking, breathing, and kicking steps for better traction, I told myself, *Relax. Don't fight it. Focus on the objective, not the distance.*

Above us, the wall narrowed to a near-vertical chute. By the time I reached the base of the chute, it was clogged with porters and donkeys. Sami muscled his way to the top first and peered back over the edge. Tossing one end of his rope down, another porter grabbed on and struggled up. Once that man was safely on top, they dropped the rope and helped the next person up.

These porters were like an army of Rambos. Since the chute was too steep and narrow even for the donkeys, they had to tie rope around each animal's belly and hoist them straight up, legs kicking midair. After all animals and porters had made it to the top, Majid climbed up. Reenergized by being so near, I came last, with Majid covering me from above.

*View looking toward Tajikistan from the top of Chilinji Pass*

We had been lucky—the weather was calm; the day sparkled with new snow. Everyone smiled, not from triumph, but relief. At first no one could talk—we were all trying to catch our breath. Then Majid grabbed a walking stick and held it like a microphone.

"Ladies and Gentlemen, good afternoon from Chilinji Pass, Pakistan, elevation 5,133 meters (16,840 feet). To the southwest is the Hindu Kush, to the west stand the Pamir, and to the northeast is the Karakoram. From here, we can see four countries: Afghanistan, Tajikistan, China, and Pakistan. This is a great day. I hope everyone is enjoying. Thank you very much!"

*A porter enjoys a cracker after reaching the top of Chilinji Pass.*

We spread out among rocks and relaxed. Even Ismail seemed perky. Only a few moments into enjoying our success, our youngest porter—no older than fifteen—collapsed. He began shaking violently and gulping air in sort, fast gasps. His body went rigid, his eyes rolled back, and he mumbled indiscernibly as saliva ran from his mouth. "Majid, come here. Something's wrong!" I shouted.

Majid ran over, along with Sami, who grabbed the boy's finger and began chanting, pausing every few seconds to spit on the boy's face. The episode spanned ten minutes, an eternity. I watched.

"Majid, this boy is epileptic," I said.

"No, what you have just witnessed is a visitation by the Fairies (angels, spirits)," Majid said, casually.

I paused, not sure what to make of this.

"But Majid, he just had a seizure!" I argued.

"No! The Fairies were communicating with him," Majid snapped, visibly annoyed. "We have many people in our culture who do this. It is quite common." Sami added something in Urdu; Majid translated: "Sami says the boy does this all the time."

"But Majid, if this happens again at the wrong time, he could die. He shouldn't be out here—he can be treated by a doctor for this," I persisted.

"No, you must understand. We believe this!" Majid shot back.

I sat with the boy until he recovered, rubbed his face with snow, and gave him water. As quickly as it had begun, the boy came out of it. He stood up and tended to our animals as though nothing ever happened.

Majid had been right; I needed to accept this.

*To his credit, a few days later Majid surprised me by saying, "I have been thinking about this. You are right, Ruth. Such people should not be allowed to trek."*

*We both had been right.*

I shifted my focus to the snow-blanketed pass, where silvery light reflected in all directions. Ahead, lay the high-altitude desert of the Karakoram.

"We have one more glacier to cross. It is only a small glacier. Do not worry," Majid said.

Actually, we were already on the glacier. New snow hid crevasses lurking just below, discernible only by subtle undulations in the snow's surface. Sami stepped cautiously, breaking trail, and seemed fully alert to the minefield he negotiated. *He knows what he's doing,* I thought, noting how he carried his sapling staff horizontally, like a tightrope walker. This would enable him to jam his staff into crevasse walls, should he break through, and hopefully, keep him from becoming trapped. Masterfully, he led the way. One by one, porters and animals lined up behind. Following a trail of blood left by our hurt donkey, I brought up the rear.

Our donkeys' sharp hooves pierced the snow, exposing black cavities, a sure sign we were crossing snow bridges, formed when wind-swept snow spans a crevasse, concealing it from view. Looking down through those perforations, I questioned whether this layer would hold. The sound of water rushing beneath meant the thin crust could give way at any time.

As we dropped in elevation, conditions didn't improve. Two rock walls had choked the glacier's downhill surge, crumpling it into a heap of ice blocks balanced so precariously that any route through them would be risky. Sami and I looked for an alternate route, he veering off to the left, where I lost sight of him.

*An ice fall on Chilinji Pass*

When Sami returned, Majid translated: "A landslide has blocked the only safe crossing over the river. We must go back up."

We turned around and began backtracking. Gradually, we made our way to a narrow passage where water blasted up geyser-like from beneath the glacier and thundered back down into a black pit. Judging by the volume, the hydraulic force had to be enormous. Over the explosive sound of water was the boom of ice blocks and boulders, slamming through passageways within the glacier. Sami searched for another crossing point and reported back to Majid. "Sami says this is the only place where we have a chance of making it across," Majid translated, in a less-than-encouraging voice. "We will cross here."

While I considered the risk of being swept off my feet and hurled beneath the ice, Sami took off his shoes and stood in front of me, waiting. He wanted me to climb onto his back.

I hesitated.

"It is only a small stream. You must trust him. He is strong enough to carry a donkey!" Majid barked.

Never underestimate terror as a motivationer. I climbed onto Sami's back, all the while thinking I should go it alone. I didn't question his strength, but carrying me would put him at risk. Fighting the water's force with me draped across his back, Sami moved clumsily. I felt every lurch, every wrench, as he stumbled and battled the current. My body tensed; the sound of rushing water filled my head. This passing by Death's door was too immediate, too hideous to consider. With every step, I tried to calculate what to do if we went down together.

*Stay focused, stay centered, and don't panic*; that's all I could do to help him.

We arrived on the opposite side. As I watched each man's struggle to cross, I relived the same deadly scenario.

"Our camp is not far from here. We will be there soon," Majid said, in a detached tone of voice. *Soon* dragged out to hours, and it was already late in the day.

It wasn't long before we were off the ice and back on firm ground. Near the interface between glacier and land stood a rock monolith covered with bright red human hand prints, a sacred site according to Majid, who went on ahead. I, however, paused to study the images. They looked as though someone had dipped their hands in red paint and clawed at the rock. I knew how those people must have felt. After so many hours of tempting fate, and defying the laws of chance, the experience now hit me. The downside risk had been real, tangible—truly terrifying by any measure.

I spotted Majid, lower down along the route, resting in a level spot. *Must be camp*, I thought. When I reached him, I plopped down, relieved to have this day behind me.

"*Inshallah*, Ruth. Now there is a problem. Here we have no food for our animals, and the one donkey is in serious condition. We must walk farther down until we find a place where the animals can graze. Camp should be just around the corner."

*In Pakistan, around the corner usually means up and over a mountain.*

We plodded on, my energy flagging. The path deteriorated to an almost indiscernible thread traversing an enormous rock slide several thousand feet in length. As we picked our way along the unstable and steep wall of rubble, my legs were heavy, like lead. I couldn't remember ever feeling so depleted. Two more hours passed before the terrain leveled out and the river broadened. We'd been on the move for fifteen hours straight. At last, Sami pointed to a cluster of boulders in the distance—camp.

"Ruth, how are you?" Majid asked.

"Grateful it ended safely," I heard myself say, almost too tired to respond.

I kicked back while our porters, seemingly unaffected by the day's events, crowded around a small fire. *What they call home is a place where daily life is measured in survival,* I thought. During the brief moment of time we had shared, we were one, together as family.

"See Ruth, now the boy is fine," Majid said, pointing to our epileptic porter. "People who communicate with the Fairies are special for us—shamans, to be exact. During our celebrations, a shaman will sometimes cut off the head of a goat and drink blood from it. Then everyone dances. Perhaps you will see this someday."

*I hope not.*

My head throbbed. We had made it back into the Karakoram. *No human will ever change this place, only survive it,* I thought. Retreating to my tent, I fell asleep, too exhausted for nightmares.

"So today we go to our pickup point," Majid said, during breakfast. "It will be flat and easy—you will love it."

*I hate it when he says things like that ...*

Our day proved anything but "flat and easy." We spent our time schlepping up and down mountainsides so steep that they ended in rivers, not valleys. But Majid's description wasn't a guide lie, of which I'd heard many. His only frame of reference was this incredibly wild bastion of nature—rugged, difficult to penetrate—with elements bigger than life, by any standard. I set new terms for myself: No more passes, no more glaciers, no more goats. No more river crossings, either.

*Returning to Hunza valley from Chilinji Pass*

The hours passed in a blur of ups, downs, rock traverses, and stomach cramps. Only the thought of the guesthouse in Karimabad kept me going. Such a welcome change it would be from camping in mud, ice, sleet, and snow. Not until sunset did a pinprick of light appear in the distance. Coming closer, a small temple-like structure, enclosed within a walled courtyard, came into view. Flags of primary colors flew along a perimeter wall, where a stockade door separated worshipers from livestock.

*Fertility shrine*

"We will camp by this shrine," Majid said. "It houses the body of a man who is special to us—what you would call a saint. People make pilgrimages here to ask favors and blessings, especially if they are having difficulty bearing children. Please, remain here while we (the men) go inside."

I found a spot among the grazing animals, sat down and waited. I had mistakenly counted on spending the night in our guesthouse in Karimabad. But no, we'd be camping with sheep instead. They sure looked dirty—hardened balls of mud hung from their wool, like Christmas ornaments, and clicked when they walked. I felt like those sheep.

When Majid exited the shrine, he shared the news: he and his wife were expecting a child. Ismail came out next, wheezing and coughing.

"Majid, we need to get him to a doctor," I said.

"Yes, Ruth. Tomorrow, in Karimabad, he will go. But now, I must buy a goat so our porters will have a safe return over the pass."

That evening, inside the cook tent, I pulled together tip money and an eclectic assortment of hats, gloves, socks, and anything I could spare for our departing porters. Outside, they lined up and waited in the dark. Despite only dim lamplight diffusing through the tent walls, I recognized each man's face, and realized with sadness this was good-bye. And how could I ever convey to Sami, our charismatic porter/leader, the comfort his strength and calm had provided?

Majid translated for me: "You are some of the strongest and bravest men I have ever known. Thank you for your friendship—I will always think of you as family." I moved down the line, taking each man's hand and speaking to him. Turning together, they disappeared into the night. A new storm hung over Chilinji Pass.

The next morning, I awoke at 4:00, but the sun didn't hit my tent until 7:00. Outside, the sky was such a deep blue, I half expected to see stars. When our departure vehicle sputtered into camp, it looked like a cross between a pickup truck and a toy wagon. I rode up front, while Majid and Ismail stayed in back. The driver hit the ignition—the engine hiccupped and died. After a quick check under the hood, our driver jumped back behind the steering wheel and tried the starter. One backfire and the engine turned over. "Pakistani system, madam," he assured me.

*I had heard this before, and it had not been reassuring.*

We rolled past fields, where hunched figures ferried loads of freshly cut hay on their backs. "We will stop here for a moment so you can watch the harvest," Majid said, as he set out across a field to greet an old woman. When the woman saw him, she hurried into her farmhouse. I thought he may have startled her, but moments later she lumbered from her front door, lugging a large bundle. Majid ran to intercept her, hoisted the load onto his shoulder, and returned to us with the package. It was wrapped in birch bark.

"This butter will ensure the good pregnancy of my wife," Majid said, carefully setting the package alongside Ismail, now coughing uncontrollably. When I saw beads of sweat covering Ismail's forehead, I pulled Majid aside: "Ismail really is sick. We need to do something."

"Yes, we will take him to the hot springs tonight," he said.

*Not exactly what I had in mind, but by now I'd learned not to press the issue.*

"Why doesn't Ismail sit in front? I can ride in back," I suggested.

Ismail waved a limp had in the negative. "Thank you, Ruth, but I think he is more comfortable where he can lie down and rest."

The next morning, despite a good night's sleep in the Hunza guesthouse, Majid showed up for breakfast looking like he'd been through a war. "I am feeling beat, and I still have this huge bump under one eye and another growing on my eyelid." Yet while he talked about his eyes, he rubbed his jaw. "I lost the tooth plug you gave me, so I had pain all night long. As soon as we get back to Islamabad, I will have to see a dentist. Tomorrow we will drive to Gilgit and fly, God willing, to Islamabad."

I asked Majid about Ismail.

"We took him to the doctor last night. The doctor gave him an injection and pills and told him to go to the hospital. But he went home instead. He has pneumonia," Majid answered.

After breakfast, I dropped into a bookstore to find a map showing Chilinji Pass. I did this despite my new conviction that in Pakistan, maps exist only for psychological benefit,

"I'm looking for a map of Chilinji Pass," I said to the shopkeeper.

"Chilinji Pass is dangerous," he responded.

"Have you been there?" I asked.

"No, and I hope never to go!" he answered, grabbing his side and groaning in pain.

"What's wrong with you?" I asked.

"Someone fell off the roof," he answered.

"Then why are you in pain?" I asked.

"He landed on top of me!" he answered.

*And he thought Chilinji was dangerous ...*

Back on the street, I met a boy who had walked all the way from Afghanistan, carrying family belongings to sell in order to take money back home. He had some ancient coins his grandfather had spent his lifetime collecting along the Silk Route. They dated back to the fourth century BC—some depicted Alexander the Great wearing a helmet made from an elephant trunk, according to the boy. Peering at the rich green patina on one coin, I managed to make out a head with a serpentine appendage rising from it.

*Circa 400 BC coin depicts Alexander the Great wearing a helmet made from an elephant trunk.*

"Your ancestors certainly were impressive," I said.

"Yes, madam, fierce warriors," he replied.

I bought his coins. Then, still not feeling well, I made a beeline back to my guesthouse.

Later that day, we left Hunza and drove south, reaching Skardu in time to board another dated aircraft for our PIA flight back to

Islamabad. "In any other country, this plane would not be allowed to fly," Majid scoffed.

Coincidently, Pakistan's one-and-only woman guide happened to be onboard. In the Islamic Republic of Pakistan, according to Majid, only men were allowed to guide. Somehow, she had broken through this barrier and several others, so it seemed—she wore jeans, sunglasses, and a denim shirt, with a veil draped casually over her shoulders. When she disappeared into the cockpit, Majid shook his head. "Now she is up there telling the pilots which buttons to push!" he muttered.

As soon as we arrived in Islamabad, Majid rushed off to the dentist. Later, he dropped by my hotel and filled me in on his day: "Yes, I had the tooth operation today. My dentist had to do a root canal and grind off my tooth. I have to go back tomorrow to have more of it fixed. My dentist wanted to know where I got the temporary filling. When I said you brought it on the trek, he was so surprised. But I told him, 'She is from an advanced culture.'"

"I'm glad you're feeling better, Majid," I said.

Majid remained silent and seemed preoccupied. At last, he spoke. "Islamabad scares me to death. I think it is one of the most dangerous places in Pakistan—I will not walk the streets after nine at night. My friend even got carjacked here! It creates trouble at home when Ziad and I have to spend time in Islamabad. Ziad's wife yells at him, and my wife gets mad at me. Arranged marriages can have problems. I told my parents, if you are going to dictate the rest of my life, you must help me out at home!"

Between his swollen eyelids, his problems at home, and his tooth, Majid was in rough shape. He sat quietly for awhile longer, and then suddenly stood up. "Well, goodnight, Ruth. I will come for you in the morning."

It was predawn when Majid picked me up for my final trip to the airport. As I left the hotel, the call to prayer ushered in daybreak—I knew I'd miss that. Majid didn't feel up to par, so once we reached the terminal, I wished him a quick good-bye and good luck with his tooth.

Inside the departure hall I slipped into the ladies room, only to discover it doubled as a money-changing operation, with matrons dealing in black market currency. After getting away from that scene, I waded through a throng of people and braced for the frantic exit procedure. I thought I'd mentally prepared myself for the security check that followed, but as all attention focused on me, my bags were dragged to the center of a crowded room and publicly torn apart. One official dashed off with both my dirty and clean laundry, while two other men disappeared with my ancient coins. Drug dogs were set loose to explore the exterior of my bags, which must have piqued their senses, scented as they were with assorted animal dung. After three more security checks, including a full-body search, I was allowed to board my flight with everything I had bought, collected, and picked up off the ground in Pakistan.

Waking up in my London hotel room between flights back to the States, I lay in bed and savored the comforts surrounding me. The sound of something being jammed under my room door distracted me—*USA Today*. PAKISTAN DEATH EDICT, read the headline plastered across the front page. A member of the Pakistan Parliament had issued a mandate: any legislator who did not vote to have Pakistan come under Islamic rule should be killed.

*It's one way to push a vote through.*

\* \* \* \* \*

October 13, 1999
*New York Times*
PAKISTAN ARMY SEIZES POWER HOURS AFTER PRIME MINISTER FIRES ARMY CHIEF

October 15, 1999
*New York Times*
PAKISTAN MILITARY COMPLETES SEIZURE OF GOVERNMENT

OCTOBER 16, 1999
*New York Times*
COUP LEADER RESTRUCTURES PAKISTAN'S GOVERNMENT

November 13, 1999
*Washington Post*
ROCKETS HIT NEAR U.S. SITES IN ISLAMABAD

"So what do you think of the headlines about Pakistan?" my husband Bob asked from behind his newspaper.

"I'm going back again someday," I answered.

"I was afraid you'd say that," he sighed.

\* \* \* \* \*

Pakistan haunted me all the years after my first two trips there. Yet with the shadow of uncertainty looming, I shifted my attention to exploring Tibet, Bhutan, Ladakh, Nepal, and Kashmir. Still, no place stood up to Pakistan.

Gripped with impatience, in 2009, I made plans to return to northern Pakistan and the glaciers surrounding K2. Unexpectedly, a new flare-up in Pakistan's Swat Valley severed communication with my Pakistani contacts. My plans fell apart. So I chose another tack—K2 from China.

*MAPS ARE APPROXIMATE

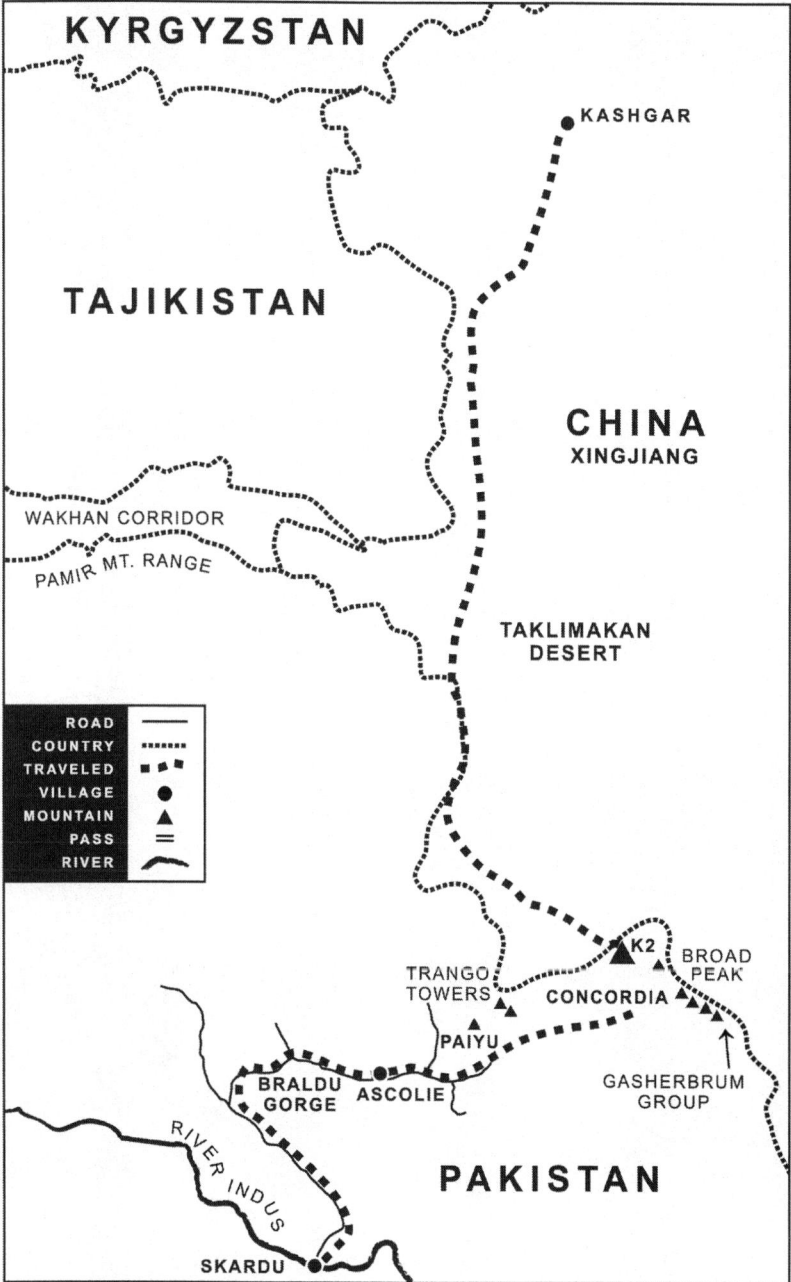

*Route traveled to K2 from Kashgar in western China*

# V.

# BACK TO K2

*Some places call to us for reasons unknown.*

## Kashgar, China

### October 2009

There are no roads to K2—no flight-seeing tours, either. K2 straddles the border between Pakistan and the Xinjiang Uygur Autonomous Region of China (Xinjiang for short), both fraught with riots, ethnic upheavals, and terrorist attacks. These days, it's a lonely place. In the fall of 2009, I returned to K2, accompanied by four Muslims (Shiite and Sunni) and three *kara buras*, the wooly black camels of Central Asia.

K2 from China is tough, beginning with the special permits required to enter the restricted military area along China's shared border with Pakistan. K2 itself is currently under Pakistani administration.

At first, it seemed doubtful whether China's Central Government would grant my visa. But after submitting a detailed dossier, my visa was issued in July of 2009. Two days later, Uyghur rioters clashed with Chinese police, leaving 170 dead in Urumqi, the capital of Xinjiang—precisely where I was going. The Uyghur people, a Turkic-speaking Muslim ethnic group, were up in arms against the Han Chinese. The Central Government responded with a lockdown of the entire Xinjiang Province (roughly thirty-five percent of the landmass of China) by imposing mandatory curfews and by cutting off Internet and phone access to Xinjiang indefinitely.

*So much for my trip*, I thought. And I still needed three more permits: one from the Chinese Mountaineering Authority, another from the Xinjiang Provincial Authority, and a third from the Chinese military. With hope of returning to K2 fading, to my great surprise, I was granted all three permits in August.

San Francisco to Beijing to Urumqi—all the way across China—in one very long day. After spending one night in Urumqi, I flew on to Kashgar, an ancient oasis empire along the Silk Road, set amidst moving sand dunes, immense mud flats, and areas, which, from the air, look like southern Utah, only bigger.

In Kashgar, Loyek, a Tajik, showed me around the old city, a medieval collection of mud buildings and narrow streets, dominated by ancestral Uyghur neighborhoods. He explained how Uyghur people originated in Turkey, hence their look—Uyghur features are more Western than Chinese. He also told me that Abdul, my Uyghur mountaineering guide, would be running a day late. The new plan: travel by jeep to the "last" Kyrgyz village, where I'd pick up my camels and begin the trek alone with only a camel driver. Abdul would catch up "soon" and continue to K2 base camp with us.

The next morning, my Uyghur escort and I began the two-day drive toward the Karakoram in a hired jeep, crossing a hot, dusty span of the Taklimakan Desert, dotted with oil wells and wind turbines. As we drove, he rattled off so many facts about the surroundings, I had to compliment him. He had picked them up from the *Lonely Planet Guide Book*, he chuckled.

The Chinese were in the process of extending the road further into the mountains. But work had only been completed to a point, beyond which there was nothing even resembling a road. This forced us to "off road" through the bottom of a dry river bed covered in rocks and boulders. The transition had little impact on our driver—he charged on without so much as letting up on the gas pedal. Obstacles seemed to come at us faster and faster—from the left, from the right—like a high-speed video game. The going was so rough that whenever we hit a bump, the radio would fly out of the dash and onto the floor. Each time this happened, our driver would let go of the wheel, steering with only his left knee, while he reached down, grabbed the radio from the floor, and jammed it back into place.

As we bounced along, I began to wonder why the Chinese bother to restrict this area. It's so tough to get to, who in their right mind would want to go there? I'm asked this frequently about my trips....

Predictably, we ended up with a flat tire. Furthermore, I had been sitting directly over the gas tank which, judging by the heavy odor of fumes, was now leaking. To make matters worse, our driver had just lit up a Chinese cigarette. We had two choices: be gassed or ignited—we were either going to arrive to our destination very quickly, or not at all. Scrambling to roll down my window, but finding no handle, I asked my driver how to open it. After stopping to change the flat, he ceremoniously pulled out his one-and-only window crank, which he kept close to his heart in his chest pocket, and rolled down every window.

Five military checkpoints later, we arrived at a cluster of mud-brick huts. When we pulled up, the entire village came out to welcome us—veiled women, men, children, even the village elder. Before I could object, they had sacrificed a ram in my honor. They honored me further by carrying the carcass into the sitting room and butchering it in front of me. The women then prepared a delicious ram pilaf.

After the feast, an older woman showed me to a pitch-dark room, deep within their enclave. I threw my sleeping bag down onto a wooden sleeping platform and crawled into it for the night. Noting a strange smell, I pulled my bag closer around my face.

As the sun rose, light began streaming in through the door to my room, along with the village chickens. Then, I spotted the odor's source—the freshly butchered ram carcass, leaning against my own sleeping platform.

*A Kyrgyz elder sports his new gift of 7eye sunglasses.*

*A Kyrgyz girl with Omar*

The village elder, also the local camel contractor, sent me off midmorning with two young men—both named Abdul—and three *kara bura* camels, which looked like giant, fur-bearing brontosauruses, with two humps instead of one. Omar (not Sharif), a big stallion, would be my camel. All day long we walked through treeless desert and parched river canyons of red sandstone and rock-and-mud conglomerate. We slogged up unstable traverses, only to give up any elevation gained by dropping back down to riverbed. Our first night, we set up camp alongside a whitewater river.

I heard chanting in the distance—the sound hung in the air and was so pleasant that I didn't need to understand the words to appreciate the spirit. My guide, Abdul, and his assistant, Rahman, had arrived.

*Kara bura camels make their way along a narrow cliff-side path before descending to a whitewater river canyon below.*

Abdul spoke "little bit English."

"Shortcut little bit dangerous," he said, the next morning, as we scrambled up a slot canyon. Shortcut, in this part of the world, usually means straight up and without a trail, which turned out to be the case. This shortcut spared us having to climb the mountain directly ahead. No kidding, dangerous—whole chunks of rock-imbedded mud broke off in my hand every time I grabbed on.

Another shortcut—this time vertical—was over an unnamed mountain, inconveniently blocking the way. At one point, I looked straight up and thought, *I can't believe we're going to climb this.* But climb we did, hand-over-hand scrambling, with plenty of exposure and without proper gear. There wasn't a disturbed rock or animal track anywhere—animals knew better. *What doesn't kill you makes you stronger,* someone once said— someone who'd never been here.

Every morning my crew of four rose at dawn, bowed to the east and knelt in prayer. Later, they chanted while we walked. At night, we celebrated the end of Ramadan, the Chinese Lunar New Year, the sixtieth anniversary of Communism in China, and we toasted to world peace. We shared what we had in common and shared what we didn't. Mostly, we shared a common goal—to reach K2.

Walking behind our kara buras for hours on end gave me plenty of time to study their feet. Instead of hooves, the undersides were smooth leather pads the size of dinner plates. With each step, the pads seemed to wrap around rocks like a catcher's mitt does a ball. They looked comfortable, and certainly more comfortable than my own feet.

After five days of spitting and barking, Omar discovered the pleasure of having his ears rubbed. He followed and nudged me, begging for more. One time, he shoved his muzzle into my soapy head of hair as I bent over washing it and then drenched me with a sneeze. A mastodon of camels, he looked like a cross between a Dr. Seuss character and something from Jurassic Park.

*I rode Omar during river crossings ... always interesting.*

During the frequent dust storms, our camels appeared ghostlike—even biblical—as they moved through the surreal and timeless desert wilderness of the Karakoram. We only encountered one tiny Kyrgyz woman tending her goats during the entire trek from the Kyrgyz village to K2 and back. Yet this lonely vastness had a meditative otherworldliness, which made me glad such places still exist.

*Abdul leads his kara bura camels through the desert wilderness to K2.*

*The only other person we saw—a Kyrgyz woman—agreed to stand with me for a photo.*

After a long traverse, the route wrapped around the mountainside and angled upward. There, at the end of a corridor framed by some of the world's highest peaks, stood K2, reclusive and unmistakable in geometry, just as I had first seen it from Pakistan. *Chugar,* locals call K2 in Kyrgyz—Great Mountain.

*High winds scour new snow from K2 after weeks of stormy weather.*

With a mantle of snow streaming from its southeast flank, K2 was still angry after weeks of violent weather—so violent, a Chinese team had failed to get beyond base camp. When we arrived, we faced the mess their team of forty-six climbers, ten cooks, and sixty camels had left behind: animal carcasses, dismembered birds, plastic bags and packaging, cigarette cartons, beer cans (some American brands)—trash everywhere we turned.

I've learned the hard way that even the best of intentions can cause loss of face in places such as this. So the next morning, I quietly began gathering trash into piles, not sure how my crew would react. But when they saw me working, they jumped in and helped. After we had base camp back in fairly good order, I thanked them.

"No, we thank you!" Abdul responded. We dragged all the trash off to the side and, as we burned it, they chanted. I asked if they'd like me to take their picture with the trash. They did, and struck poses conveying importance, clearly proud of the difference they'd made.

By evening, the mountain had calmed. I found a boulder, sat alone and watched K2 meld into the night sky. And I thought, *What a lesser place our world would be without this. And how much less I would have lived my own life had I not come back here.*

*K2 viewed from China base camp*